T0235926

IFIP Advances in Information and Communication Technology 588

Editor-in-Chief

Kai Rannenberg, Goethe University Frankfurt, Germany

Editorial Board Members

TC 1 – Foundations of Computer Science
  Luís Soares Barbosa(i), University of Minho, Braga, Portugal
TC 2 – Software: Theory and Practice
  Michael Goedicke, University of Duisburg-Essen, Germany
TC 3 – Education
  Arthur Tatnall(i), Victoria University, Melbourne, Australia
TC 5 – Information Technology Applications
  Erich J. Neuhold, University of Vienna, Austria
TC 6 – Communication Systems
  Burkhard Stiller, University of Zurich, Zürich, Switzerland
TC 7 – System Modeling and Optimization
  Fredi Tröltzsch, TU Berlin, Germany
TC 8 – Information Systems
  Jan Pries-Heje, Roskilde University, Denmark
TC 9 – ICT and Society
  David Kreps(i), University of Salford, Greater Manchester, UK
TC 10 – Computer Systems Technology
  Ricardo Reis(i), Federal University of Rio Grande do Sul, Porto Alegre, Brazil
TC 11 – Security and Privacy Protection in Information Processing Systems
  Steven Furnell(i), Plymouth University, UK
TC 12 – Artificial Intelligence
  Eunika Mercier-Laurent(i), University of Reims Champagne-Ardenne, Reims, France
TC 13 – Human-Computer Interaction
  Marco Winckler(i), University of Nice Sophia Antipolis, France
TC 14 – Entertainment Computing
  Rainer Malaka, University of Bremen, Germany

IFIP – The International Federation for Information Processing

IFIP was founded in 1960 under the auspices of UNESCO, following the first World Computer Congress held in Paris the previous year. A federation for societies working in information processing, IFIP's aim is two-fold: to support information processing in the countries of its members and to encourage technology transfer to developing nations. As its mission statement clearly states:

IFIP is the global non-profit federation of societies of ICT professionals that aims at achieving a worldwide professional and socially responsible development and application of information and communication technologies.

IFIP is a non-profit-making organization, run almost solely by 2500 volunteers. It operates through a number of technical committees and working groups, which organize events and publications. IFIP's events range from large international open conferences to working conferences and local seminars.

The flagship event is the IFIP World Computer Congress, at which both invited and contributed papers are presented. Contributed papers are rigorously refereed and the rejection rate is high.

As with the Congress, participation in the open conferences is open to all and papers may be invited or submitted. Again, submitted papers are stringently refereed.

The working conferences are structured differently. They are usually run by a working group and attendance is generally smaller and occasionally by invitation only. Their purpose is to create an atmosphere conducive to innovation and development. Refereeing is also rigorous and papers are subjected to extensive group discussion.

Publications arising from IFIP events vary. The papers presented at the IFIP World Computer Congress and at open conferences are published as conference proceedings, while the results of the working conferences are often published as collections of selected and edited papers.

IFIP distinguishes three types of institutional membership: Country Representative Members, Members at Large, and Associate Members. The type of organization that can apply for membership is a wide variety and includes national or international societies of individual computer scientists/ICT professionals, associations or federations of such societies, government institutions/government related organizations, national or international research institutes or consortia, universities, academies of sciences, companies, national or international associations or federations of companies.

More information about this series at http://www.springer.com/series/6102

Eunika Mercier-Laurent (Ed.)

Artificial Intelligence for Knowledge Management

6th IFIP WG 12.6 International Workshop, AI4KM 2018
Held at IJCAI 2018
Stockholm, Sweden, July 15, 2018
Revised and Extended Selected Papers

 Springer

Editor
Eunika Mercier-Laurent (iD)
University of Reims Champagne-Ardenne
Saint Drezery, France

ISSN 1868-4238   ISSN 1868-422X (electronic)
IFIP Advances in Information and Communication Technology
ISBN 978-3-030-52905-5   ISBN 978-3-030-52903-1 (eBook)
https://doi.org/10.1007/978-3-030-52903-1

© IFIP International Federation for Information Processing 2020
This work is subject to copyright. All rights are reserved by the Publisher, whether the whole or part of the material is concerned, specifically the rights of translation, reprinting, reuse of illustrations, recitation, broadcasting, reproduction on microfilms or in any other physical way, and transmission or information storage and retrieval, electronic adaptation, computer software, or by similar or dissimilar methodology now known or hereafter developed.
The use of general descriptive names, registered names, trademarks, service marks, etc. in this publication does not imply, even in the absence of a specific statement, that such names are exempt from the relevant protective laws and regulations and therefore free for general use.
The publisher, the authors and the editors are safe to assume that the advice and information in this book are believed to be true and accurate at the date of publication. Neither the publisher nor the authors or the editors give a warranty, expressed or implied, with respect to the material contained herein or for any errors or omissions that may have been made. The publisher remains neutral with regard to jurisdictional claims in published maps and institutional affiliations.

This Springer imprint is published by the registered company Springer Nature Switzerland AG
The registered company address is: Gewerbestrasse 11, 6330 Cham, Switzerland

Preface

The IJCAI 2018 program was more diversified than the previous, covering quite a number of fields in artificial intelligence (AI) (https://www.ijcai.org/proceedings/2018/). We did not find knowledge management (KM) but the main conference included some of its components such as knowledge representation, dynamics of knowledge, knowledge base, knowledge transfer, shared knowledge, knowledge engineering, visual knowledge, and combining knowledge with deep convolutional neural networks.

Understanding the benefits of KM for research, organizations, and businesses, and then applying it, is still a challenge for many. The overall process involving people, big data, and all kinds of computers and applications has the potential to accelerate discovery and innovation from an organized and optimized flow of knowledge. This collection of selected, extended, and updated articles aims in challenging researchers and practitioners in better exploring all AI fields and integrating world feedback from experience.

KM is a large multidisciplinary field having its roots in management and AI. AI brought a way of thinking, knowledge modeling, knowledge processing, and problem-solving techniques. Knowledge is one of intangible capitals that influence the performance of organizations and their capacity to innovate. Since the beginning of the KM movement in the early nineties, companies and nonprofit organizations have experimented various approaches.

After the first AI4KM (Artificial Intelligence for Knowledge Management) was organized by IFIP (International Federation for Information Processing) group TC12.6 (Knowledge Management) in partnership with ECAI (European Conference on Artificial Intelligence) in 2012 and the second workshop was held during the Federated Conferences on Computer Science and Information Systems (Fedcsis 2014) in conjunction with Knowledge Acquisition and Management conference (KAM), the third manifestation began a partnership with IJCAI (International Joint Conference on Artificial Intelligence) since in 2015. The 4th AI4KM was held in New York (IJCAI 2016) and the 5th in Melbourne, Australia, co-located with IJCAI 2017.

The objective of this multidisciplinary conjunction is still to raise interest of AI researchers and practitioners in KM challenges, to discuss methodological, technical, and organizational aspects of AI used for KM and to share the feedback on KM applications using AI.

We would like to thank the members of the Program Committee, who reviewed the papers and helped put together an interesting program in Stockholm. We would also like to thank all authors and our invited talk by Prof. Helena Lindskog from Linkoping University. Finally, our thanks go out to the Local Organizing Committee and all the supporting institutions and organizations.

This volume contains the selection, updated, and extended papers presented during the workshop. The selection focused on new contributions in any research area concerning the use of all AI fields for KM. An extended Program Committee then evaluated the last versions of the proposals, leading to this volume.

Our invited talk by Prof. Helena Lindskog from Linkoping University, Sweden, addressed a timely topic: "Globalization - Understanding the Correlations Between Attitudes Towards Globalization, Time, Resources and Financial Resources." Paradoxically, we have an increasing amount of technology supposed to help us and allow for more time, but the results are the opposite – we have less time. How can AI help in being "time rich"?

The next article presents the latest thesis work on "Integrated System for Students' Evaluation Using KM Approach." It describes a KM approach to the evaluation of international students' profiles. Based on AI techniques the proposed system aims in providing accurate evaluation of candidates considering also their cultural background, behaviors, and wishes. It explores existing expertise in this field.

Collaboration of SME is a condition for survival. The authors of "ICT Platform Design for SME Collaboration" propose to define a conceptual platform for functional and process flows in discrete complex manufacturing industries.

Another "Platform for Knowledge Society and Innovation Ecosystems" aims in fulfilling the very important hidden need – having a digital place grouping world knowledge related to innovation. The current pandemic of COVID-19 highlights the necessity of grouping world research on the topic to be more effective in managing the crisis.

The authors of the next paper "Measuring Successful Digital Services by Identifying Active Users" propose applying KM approach to evaluate the success of digital services. Compared to traditional methods they present an alternative and innovative method of "understanding" the user satisfaction from his/her activity.

"Effective Management of Information Processes with CMS in Smart City. The Concept of Crowdsourcing" describes some principles of sustainable managing a smart city and the related flow of knowledge. The proposed Resident Portal aims in fully coordinated and properly managed communication between residents, stakeholders, and municipal authorities. Such a portal enchance collaborative innovation of all stakeholders.

The next paper entitled "A Naming System for "The Internet of Things" Adapted to Industry - A Case Study in Electrical Engineering" points out the difficulty of comprehensive naming of processes and associated functions in digitalization of industry. The authors propose cognitive representations of these processes with focus on the denomination of computer objects in relation to their real-world correspondence and the functional representation within the information systems.

"Augmented Learning and Data Filtering: Knowledge Management and Discovery" describes designing predictive modeling of strategic decision systems with applications to analytics, enterprise modeling, and cognitive social media business interfaces. The areas explored range from plan goal decision tree satisfiability with competitive business models to predictive analytics models that accomplish goals on a three tier glimpse to business systems.

Focus on education, the authors of "A Note on Knowledge Management Education: Towards Implementing Active Learning Methods" present useful teaching methods in active education, especially oriented towards courses where innovation and delivering dynamic knowledge are critical. The goal of the paper is to present and discuss criteria relevant in the selection of active educational methods supporting KM courses.

We invited Konstantin M. Golubev, working on original "Intellect Modelling Kit." The intellect modeling aims to amplify of human intellect and is an alternative to traditional AI. The goal is to assist human intellect on every step of its activity, accept human knowledge, and develop new knowledge together with people. The activity of intellect modeling applications could be verified by human expert on every stage.

We hope you will enjoy reading these papers.

May 2020   Eunika Mercier-Laurent

Organization

Editor

Eunika Mercier-Laurent   University of Reims Champagne Ardenne, France

Program Committee

Danielle Boulanger	University of Lyon 3, France
Anne Dourgnon	EDF Research Center, France
Otthein Hertzog	Jacobs University, Germany
Knut Hinkelmann	University of Applied Sciences and Arts, Switzerland
Gülgün Kayakutlu	Istanbul Technical University, Turkey
Antoni Ligeza	AGH, University of Science and Technology, Poland
Helena Lindskog	Linköping University, Sweden
Nada Matta	Troyes Technical University, France
Eunika Mercier-Laurent	University of Reims Champagne Ardenne, France
Mieczyslaw Lech Owoc	Wroclaw University of Economics, Poland
Abdul Sattar	Griffith University, Australia
Frederique Segond	Inria, France
Guillermo Simari	Universidad Nacional del Sur, Argentina
Janusz Wojtusiak	George Mason University, USA

Local Organizing Committee

Eunika Mercier-Laurent	University of Reims Champagne Ardenne, France
Kevin Leyton-Brown	The University of British Columbia, Canada
Helena Lindskog	Linköping University, Sweden

Contents

Globalization - Understanding the Correlations Between Attitudes Towards Globalization, Time, Resources and Financial Resources

Helena Lindskog$^{(\boxtimes)}$

Department of Management and Economics, Institute of Technology,
University of Linköping, Linköping, Sweden
helli@eki.liu.se

Abstract. Reinforced by AI e-marketing is now an established, important and often decisive channel especially for B2C (business to consumer) activities. One of the visible characteristics of today's world is globalization. In developed societies where services, products and possibilities abound, not only money but increasingly time is becoming an important value. People's availability of time is crucial for how they work, form their lives and how they act when choosing, buying and using products in the market place. The attitudes towards globalization influence not only choices of products and services but also the way people use Internet and accept it as a marketing channel for exposure for known and new for them products and services and brands. Therefore, time & money resources and attitudes towards globalization are also decisive for companies in development of products and services, and marketing of them. Artificial Intelligence has a great role to play in time optimization.

Keywords: Globalization · Time-Rich · Time-Poor · Artificial Intelligence · Knowledge management · Technology · E-commerce

1 Introduction

Time has always been of interest in many fields: physics, social science, management, information processing, manufacturing, logistics, cooking and many others. Internet has contributed to the process of globalization and has shaken our relation to time. Various applications aiming in helping humans track also our navigation including eye tracking. AI algorithms explore these files and marketing overrun us with ads and emails proposing the products, and services that mostly we do not need. Paradoxically instead of having more time, we have less, but we can have more. Condition however is the different thinking and development of smart and green IT powered by AI and wise organization of related knowledge.

The aim of the presented work is the understanding the correlations between attitudes toward globalization, time resource and financial resource.

Developed countries including those with accelerated development influenced by globalization are affluent societies having most physical needs in sense of Maslow satisfied [6]. The poorer segments are comparatively rich in a historical perspective and as such, they are interesting as consumer groups. There is still a divide regarding wealth

© IFIP International Federation for Information Processing 2020
Published by Springer Nature Switzerland AG 2020
E. Mercier-Laurent (Ed.): AI4KM 2018, IFIP AICT 588, pp. 1–13, 2020.
https://doi.org/10.1007/978-3-030-52903-1_1

and spending capacity, but we also experience digital divide and time divide. From a consumer perspective, all are important. The *time divide* between those groups that are *time-poor* and those that are *time-rich* makes a difference in their way of buying. Largely there is a high positive correlation between a high degree of wealth and time-poverty as well as the opposite (a new situation in a historical setting [8].

The degree of time poverty or time pressure is an important aspect of consumer behaviour and an important variable in market segmentation for consumer goods and services. Time-poor buying and also consumption behaviour is focused upon "saving time" and time-rich buying and consumption behaviour is more focused upon "killing time".

Already in the 1960s, the Swedish economist Staffan Burenstam-Linder pointed out in his book "The Hurried Leisure Class" [1] that consumption in an affluent society is limited by our scarcest resource: *time*. He demonstrated that the mechanism behind time-poverty depends on the increasing amount of products in the market. His predictions such as increasing prosperity is not giving us *"... peace and harmony... in reality it is in this case in contrary. The pace increases and life becomes more hectic."* [1] are now becoming evident. Globalization has influenced the increase of products and services dramatically and it continues. The trend of planned obsolescence and accelerated innovation in packaging and "new" standards make the consumer lost while searching for a favourite product. Burenstam-Linder consideration *"...not only production but also consumption demands time"* are valid today and will be in the future.

More recently, Paul Romer, professor of economics at Stanford University explained: *"The decline in the cost of IT hardware has been so rapid that it's tempting to assume it explains all the changes that take place in the economy and society. But in our lifetime, we've witnessed a second price change that's as jolting as the one in hardware: The cost of time has increased. To be sure, the rate of increase in the cost of time has been much less dramatic than the rate of price declines in IT. But human time is used in every productive process and every consumption activity, so changes in the cost of time have pervasive effects on the economy and society"* [11].

However, not all consumer groups are time-poor. After fulfilling the basic needs some have time and money to spend upon other kinds of need fulfillment, social exchange and self-actualization, at higher levels of the Maslow's hierarchy of needs [6]. The entertainment as music, television and games could be very time consuming. The consumption patterns of young generations change with ubiquitous connections. Are they time-rich or time-poor?

The information society and especially the Internet has opened new ways of consumption via e-commerce and m-commerce. Navigation and "customer experience" data explored by AI techniques allows spreading advertisements on products and services. Closing the ads windows of not interesting ones and waiting mandatory time on videos takes time. The digital divide between groups who use the Internet and those who do not is not equal to the time divide. We find groups using the Internet and e-commerce that are time-poor and other groups that are time-rich and we think that using time, as a segmentation variable is equally important in e-commerce.

The purpose of this article is to clarify the concepts of time-poor and time-rich and to discuss its usefulness for market segmentation of consumer behaviours, especially in the context of globalization, ubiquitous pushing to buy and exploring "client experience". This is a conceptual paper identifying different consumer situations and market segments. To verify our theoretical models and hypotheses it will be necessary to complement them by statistics and experiments.

2 Time-Rich and Time-Poor – Consumer Segmentation Approach

One of marketing methods for increasing the precision in marketing management is market segmentation [4]. It is the process of defining and subdividing a large homogenous market into clearly identifiable segments having similar needs, wants, or demand characteristics. Furthermore, in order to be a useful the segments should be identifiable and measurable.

According to Skiffman and Kanuk [12] there are several bases for segmentation:

- Geographic (region, city size, density, climate)
- Demographic (age, gender, marital status, income, education, occupation)
- Psychological (needs, personality, perception, attitude, learning-involvement)
- Sociocultural (culture, religion, social class)
- Usage (heavy, medium, light; awareness, loyalty)
- Situation (time, objective, location, social)
- Lifestyle (psychographics, VALS-achievers, believers, strugglers; active/passive, social/hermit)
- Benefit (convenience, social acceptance/status, economy/value)
- Hybrid segmentation (demographic/psychographic: profiles of consumer segments, SRIVALS-fulfilled, experiencer, striver; geodemographics: characteristics of neighbourhoods; demographic/technology).

2.1 Macro-segmentation Based on Demographic and Geographic Variables

A first approximation of time-poor and time-rich market segments could be found in a macro-segmentation based in first step on demographic variables and in a second step complemented with geographic variables. This macro-segmentation could most of all give us an indication of the "overall time pressure" on consumer behaviour of different consumer segments. Demographic variables are age, family status and employment status.

Time-Rich Market Segment
The time-rich are people/consumers with the perception that time abounds and they often associate with "killing time". This group is large, larger than in any other period of human history. However, only a fraction of the time-rich is also money-rich. This group contains the following socio-economic segments:

- Retired people
- Children and youth
- Unemployed

The main reason for having such a large group of Time-Rich are:

- increased prosperity
- retirement with pension
- longer life
- no child work

To be retired with a comfortable pension is a new idea in a historical perspective. The number of retired people with pension is increasing rapidly. Life expectancy is also constantly increasing. In all this is an increasingly interesting segment from a commercial perspective.

In most countries, the law forbids child-work and due to the longer studies, the work debut is for every year becoming later. Many young people study and many are postponing their family and work responsibilities much longer than just a generation ago.

The unemployed are also time-rich and fluctuate between time-rich and time-poor depending on the state of the economy.

Time-Poor Market Segment

Most professionals and parents with small children are time-poor. Many of the time-poor perceive time as their scarcest resource and the term "saving time" is often associated with time-poor. The main reasons for having such a large group of time-poor are:

- those employed have to work hard freely or as consequence of organizational pressure
- the distinction between work and leisure is becoming more blurred
- the increasing supply of goods, services and choices to fill up our time
- the need to always be prepared for changes, to learn and acquire new knowledge
- the consciousness that you yourself are in charge and responsible for your future.

The Attraction of Work

Time-poverty is often associated with economic success in the affluent societies. Work identity is for many becoming more and more important. In addition, work itself has become more exciting. It gives new challenges every day and a big dose of satisfaction. Anthropologist Jan English-Lueck, expresses it this way: *"We call it techno-optimism. There is an addiction to opportunity and if you don't see it that way, why are you even here?"* [9]. Although the time-rich group is equally large, most of the interest in media is devoted to the time-poor.

Work and Leisure

We are used to go to job, work there, then go home from work and be free for leisure activities, to relax, to be with family and friends, go fishing etc. Our time has been divided between work and non-work or leisure activities. The intention with home or distance work is meant to be good, but it often results in both long hours at work combined with early or late working hours at home. The information technology and telecommunications give us all the possibility to work and get in touch with the office anywhere, anytime and soon even anyway. Only a few people can avoid the temptation to check the voice and e-mail messages when they are out of their office if they have the possibility to do that.

Supply and Choices to Fill Up Our Time
We have never before had so many choices of goods, services and activities and we must constantly take decisions at home, at work and other places. Possessions demand more time than we realize. If we buy a smartphone, camera, a pair of skis, a food robot or a hundred other similar items, we will also like to use them. These items are supposed to make our life easier, but instead they occupy space and need to be looked after. Sometimes, our possessions seem to demand us to use them. "Promulgators of the 24-h society begin by identifying (correctly) two themes of modern life; first a consumerist hunger designed to be unappeasable, and second a time-sickness at the heart of an over-hurried society; too much to do, too little time" [2].

Need to Always Be Prepared for Changes, to Learn and Acquire New Knowledge
The technical development goes very fast and speed is likely to accelerate. Due also to planned obsolescence we have to change devices, learn new interfaces, Technology as for example AI changes professions, requires new knowledge, and know how. Today's way of working in some fields will be obsolete tomorrow. Life-long learning is not only a buzzword. It is in most of professions becoming a necessity.

You Are Yourself Responsible for Your Future
Your decisions can change your situation. It is important to meet the right people and to have the right education, be slim nice looking and tanned (in northern countries), wear the fashionable clothes, read the right magazines, be visible on the right social networks and be creative with new ideas in time that can be keys for success in the professional and social life. Many preach Carpe Diem. However, it is not easy to combine all of mentioned with the responsibility for your own future.

Complementary Geographic Segmentation – Living in Large Metropolitan Areas or Less Urban
We think that the macro-segmentation approach also should include a complementary geographical distinction between consumer groups living in large metropolitan areas or less urban. The reason is obvious, living in large cities most certainly adds to the time-poverty. First of all transportation to and from work etc. takes more time and secondly probably time-poor people have less of supporting networks from family and friends.

   Our **hypothesis** is that e-commerce regarding conventional goods could primarily be regarded as large metropolitan phenomena. Empirical evidence from the Swedish horizon also points in that direction (at least so far).

2.2   Micro-segmentation – What Does Lifestyle Add to Our Understanding?

Our first approximation of time-rich and time-poor market segments based upon demographic and geographic variables need to be further complemented both in our understanding of the overall time pressure and also in our understanding of the time pressure felt in each specific purchasing or consumption situation.

Lifestyle segmentation could give us further information of the priorities of different groups at an overall level and also regarding specific situations of purchasing and consumption. The crucial question is if belonging to different lifestyles differentiates between time-poverty and time-richness. First, let us look at a common lifestyle segmentation, VALS^{TM} (Values and Lifestyles) that categorises U.S. adult consumers into mutually exclusive groups based on their psychology and several key demographic [15].

Using the self-orientation and resources dimensions, VALS defines eight segments of adult consumers who have different attitudes and exhibit distinctive behavior and decision-making patterns. Neighboring types have similar characteristics and can be combined for analysis as primary and secondary types.

The eight segments are following:

1. **Strugglers** have minimal resources; practical, self-sufficient, like to work with their hands, value things with a functional purpose such as tools and utility vehicles, tend to hunt and fish more than the general population.
2. **Actualizers** have abundant resources; conventional; politically conservative; social lives revolve around family, church and career; work provides status, material success and sense of duty; tend to own swimming pools.
3. **Fulfilleds** are higher income and principle oriented; young, enthusiastic, seek variety and excitement; into sports and social activities; spend money on fast food, clothes, movies, music; likely to have attended rock concert in past year.
4. **Achievers** are higher income and status oriented; money defines success; concerned about opinions of others; trying to find their place in life but may feel unsure of themselves; want to be stylish and own high-status possessions.
5. **Experiencers** are higher income and action oriented; successful, affluent, active, high self-esteem, interested in expressing themselves in different ways; often leaders yet seek new challenges; tendency for foreign travel, dinner parties and the arts.
6. **Believers** are lower income and principle oriented; poor, elderly, low education, concerned about health, cautious; may feel resigned and passive about life; worried about security and safety; may not buy much but are loyal to their favorite brands.
7. **Strivers** are lower income and status oriented; conventional, conservative, predictable; strong, fixed beliefs and rules of conduct about church, family, community and nation; modest incomes and education but sufficient to meet their needs.
8. **Makers** are lower income and action oriented; mature, reflective; well educated, well informed and value knowledge; professional occupations; while respecting order, also open to new ideas and change in society; want durability and functionality in what they buy.

Looking at the lifestyle segmentation above, you could conclude that it is rather difficult to classify these segments as being either time-poor or time-rich at the overall level. If degree of time-poverty most closely equals degree of economic wealth, then time-rich segment are Strugglers (1), Believers (6) and Strivers (7) and Makers (8). Time-poor segments are Fulfilleds (3), Achievers (4), Experiencers (5) and Actualisers (2). Most difficult to position are Actualizers (2) and Makers (8).

In our opinion, this connection is valid between time-poverty and abundance of resources.

Nevertheless, you could also speculate if the principle oriented Fulfilleds (3) and Believers (6) are less time-poor compared to the status oriented Achievers (4) and Strivers (7) and especially compared to the action oriented Experiencers (5) and Makers (8). On an overall level, these questions of differences between lifestyle groups have to be further investigated when it comes to the overall degree of time-poverty.

What is more important to conclude is that different lifestyle groups give priority to different consumption patterns and consequently also express time-richness and time-poverty in different specific consumer situations. Therefore, lifestyle could be a valuable basis for segmentation for specific products according to time-richness or time-poverty (Fig. 1).

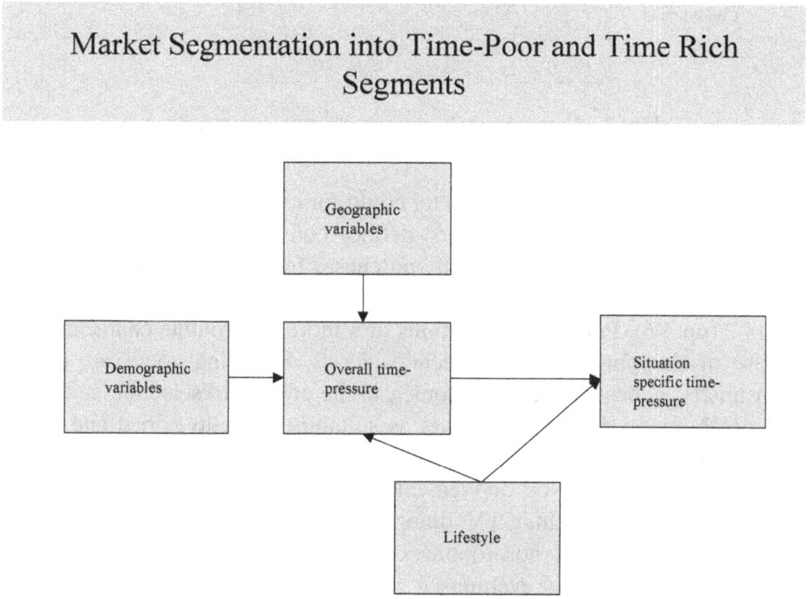

Fig. 1. Market segmentation into time-rich and time-poor segments

3   Time-Rich and Time-Poor Consumer Behavior

In this article, we use the concept of consumer behavior in an overall meaning. According to Kotler [5] consumer behavior can be divided into buying behavior and consumption behavior. Another starting point is the distinction between routine and non-routine behavior, which is in focus of the buy class model [10].

3.1   A Classification of Different Consumer Situations

If we combine the distinctions between buying and consumption and routine and non-routine, we end up in the following matrix.

Consumer Behavior - A Classification Matrix

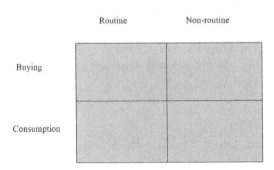

Fig. 2. Consumer behavior - a classification matrix

Situations that are of a routine character could for example be the daily and weekly buying of convenience goods. Kotler [5] defines convenience goods as "those consumers' goods which the customer usually purchases frequently, immediately and with a minimum of effort in comparison and buying (examples. Tobacco products, soap, newspapers)" (pp. 96). Purchasing situations of a more non-routine character could be the purchase of shopping goods or specialty goods. Shopping goods are defined as "those consumers' goods which the customer, in the process of selection and purchase, characteristically compares on such bases as suitability, quality, price and style (examples: furniture, dress goods, used automobiles and major appliances)" [5, pp. 96].

Consumption could also be divided into routine and non-routine. Examples of routine consumption are watching TV, doing banking services and cooking during the working week. Examples of non-routine consumption are vacations, going to the theater and cooking for Friday evenings.

Time-poor purchasing and consumption behavior have some common characteristics:

- "Do it as fast as possible" - going to the nearest shopping mall or doing the purchasing over the internet or when it comes to consumption to slip into a fast food restaurant for lunch etc.
- "Do it when suitable" - doing shopping or bank services over the Internet at ten in the evening etc.
- "Don't do it at all, let someone else do it" - buying services for shopping or cleaning the house or getting help from family members that are more time-rich etc.

Time-rich purchasing and consumption have other characteristics such as:

- "Let the process take time for social purposes, learning and self-improvement" - shopping is also a social event for instance buying clothes together with friends, fixing the house by yourself could be very satisfying etc.

- "Killing time", i.e. watching TV or listening to music when you don't have anything else to do etc.

Regarding the use of e-commerce we see the time-rich and time-poor behavior in all four consumer situations, a statement that will be elaborated later on in this article.

3.2 What is the Proper Unit of Analysis?

The unit of analysis for consumption could be at either the individual level or the aggregate family level. Individuals could be time-poor, but collectively the family could be regarded as time rich with children and retired elderly taking part in the buying and consumption processes.

Households/families can be divided into:

- only time-poor
- only time-rich
- mixed: time-rich and time-poor

If a family/household is a mixed one with both time-rich and time-poor members as well as if every member of the family/household has access to the Web and online shopping it can lead to new buying patterns.

In the mixed family/household time-rich can not only perform shopping activities for themselves but also serve as human agents for the time-poor members of the family/household. Already today, some parents ask their more time-rich children for example to find out the evening cinema program or sport activities and book tickets. Perhaps in the future to be a human agent will be one of the most important tasks for a majority of grandmas and grandpas. Their available time for bargain hunting, investigations and participation in various communities will be of a great value to the others. However some are already replaced with electronic assistants.

4 Online Shopping

4.1 Web Characteristics

Prof. Donna L. Hoffman from George Washington School of Business, in her presentation February 9, 2001, at UCLA research conference pointed out what makes the Web different:

- Many-to-many communication model
- Interactivity with both people and computers
- Environment approaches full information
- The customer has much greater control
- Allows unprecedented level of choice
- Customer competence is an issue
- An alternate to, rather than a simulation of, the "real world"
- Experiential and goal-directed activities are juxtaposed

Prof. Donna L. Hoffman also pointed out that the successful implementation of an online commerce with a Value Model must address the four Digital Desiderata:

- **Useability** - ease of use
- **Doability** - intuitive navigation, "getting around," easy moves, searchable, fast
- **Endless frontier** - discovery, vast pool of information, serendipity
- **Human touch** - trust, community, personalization

Her current research is on consumer behavior in online environments and on social commerce [16].

4.2   Goal-Oriented and Experiential Shopping

The consumers shop both on-line and off-line for goal-oriented (for efficiency and to save time) or experiential (for fun and to kill time) reasons. Several factors for on-line shopping differ from off-line shopping due to uniqueness of the Web.

Prof. Mary Wolfinbarger from the California State University Long Beach and prof. Mary Gilly from University of California in their paper on "Shopping Online for Freedom, Control and Fun" [13] present the results from the focus group on online shopping. The results of their research point out that the majority of the shoppers are goal-oriented.

Why are more e-tailing consumers expected to be goal-focused? One clue is the finding that time starved consumers are especially likely to be online shoppers. Another clue is that early and heavy users of the Internet tend to have strong internal locus for control, and thus are goal-oriented personalities.

Our research with online shoppers suggests that goal-oriented shoppers are interested in e-tailing because of four specific attributes: (1) convenience and accessibility (2) selection (3) availability of information and (4) lack of sociality. Importantly, shoppers frequently and explicitly associate these goal- oriented attributes with increased freedom and control.

Why are some online shoppers engaging in experiential behavior? Experiential shoppers tell us they enjoy (1) auctions (2) involvement with hobby/product class and (3) bargain hunting: in sum, these shoppers focus on "the experience" or fun of online shopping as much as they do on product acquisitions [13].

The results of this investigation are summarised in Table 1.

Table 1. Goal-oriented and experiential factors and outcomes of online shopping [13]

	Important factors	Outcome desired
Goal-oriented shopping	Accessibility/convenience Selection Information availability Lack of sociality	Freedom Control Commitment to goal Not experience
Experiential shopping	Involvement with product class Positive sociality Positive surprise Bargain hunting	Fun Commitment to experience as important or more important than goal

4.3   Implications for E-Commerce and Time-Rich/Time-Poor Consumer Behaviour

Online shoppers' motivations that can be divided into two main groups are very much correlated with the distinction between time-rich and time-poor. Time-poor buying behaviour is goal-oriented and that goes for both routine and non-routine (cf. Fig. 2). Goal oriented and routine buying behaviour executed by time-poor consumers could be buying railway tickets or groceries over the internet. If e-commerce is the best alternative among all time-poor solutions is perhaps not as easy to say. For instance buying a railway ticket could be more time-efficiently done, by picking up the phone and calling the travel agency, but at a higher cost. Also non-routine buying of shopping and special character could be very time-efficiently done over the internet. Compared to other media, the internet could offer a very efficient search process and a vast array of offerings which could be analysed in a rational mode.

Time-rich buying behaviour is very similar to the experiential mode as mentioned above and that could also be applicable in both routine and non-routine situations. Of course the non-routine situation is mostly in focus. Bargain hunting could cover both routine and non-routine depending on what kind of consumer goods we are dealing with. But experiential and non-routine on-line shopping is also for fun and a learning experience. To sum up the buying part of consumer behaviour on the Internet, Lindskog [7] gives the following characteristics of time-poor and time-rich buying behaviours:

Time-poor

– Proposals - ready to make decision
– Perception of being chosen by proposals especially combined for you
– Feeling of having the possibility to check any detail if needed
– Saving time
– Relief of problems
– Agents

Time-rich

– Each purchase should be a bargain
– Possibility to make own comparisons and combinations
– "Mediterranean market"
– Delivery time adapted to price chosen by supplier
– Important information source for the time-poor
– Time-rich can easily inform the whole world if they are not satisfied

We also think that the difference between goal-oriented and experiential is valid for the distinction between time-poor and time-rich consumption. Especially, we see a correlation between goal-orientation and routine consumption of e-services such as banking services or watching the development on the stock exchange in real-time. We also propose a strong correlation between time-rich consumption and experiential behavior, such as the loading down of entertainment from the Internet.

5   Final Remarks and Implications for Further Research

From a marketing point of view, the basic question is if the design of the customer offerings as well as the choice of e-commerce as a marketing channel are well adapted to different consumers' actual situations and perceptions expressed in terms of time-richness or time-poverty? When we talk about services of the Internet the service and the marketing channel seem almost inseparable.

– How much time is the consumer willing to invest in information seeking and comparison of alternatives? Internet as a marketing channel has many features well adapted to time-poor decision making. To begin with, it provides comparatively quick information seeking and comparison between alternatives. Several Internet services are designed to improve these parts of consumer decision-making, for example information brokerage when buying a used car. But the Internet is also a very interesting marketing channel towards the time-rich, surfing over the net and taking part in different communities.

– How much time is the consumer willing to spend on the actual buying activities and at what time of the day? Again, the comparative success of Internet banking is due to the fact that this marketing channel is perfectly adapted to a time-poor consumption pattern, more quickly executed and more flexible in time (24-h availability). Buying groceries over the Internet is another area, which so far has not proven especially successful (at least not in Sweden). There are many explanation to this failure – from bad execution from the seller side regarding web sites, deliveries etc. to consumers not being willing to pay extra for home deliveries. One explanation is also that not so many consumers are time-poor at the family level, especially not when we look outside the large cities.

Questions for further research ranges from providing the theoretical concepts of time-poor and time-rich with empirical data to prove their validity to classifying consumer behaviours and e-commerce and a to go further into time as an important variable to explain consumer patterns and success and failure in e-commerce.

Artificial intelligence modified the speed of market analysis by offering a possibility of mining marketing Big Data. While collecting data about consumer navigation and purchase online is easy, the main marketing approach did not evolved. It is still pushing goods to consumer instead of innovating with them. If only we could have more intelligent e-commerce able to say immediately "we have or we don't have" instead of going through categories of products it will help being more time-rich.

This article is adapted from "The Importance of Time-rich and Time-poor Consumer Behaviour for the E-commerce" by Helena Lindskog and Staffan Brege (https://www.researchgate.net/publication/267954913_The_Importance_of_Time-rich_and_Time-po or_Consumer_Behavior_for_the_E-commerce) *and updated.*

References

1. Burenstam-Linder, S.: Den rastlösa välfärdsmänniskan, Tidsbrist i överflöd – en ekonomisk studie, Bonniers (1969)
2. Griffiths, J.: Colonising the Night. Red Pepper, May 2000
3. Hoffman, D.: Consequences of the web for customers and firms: developing a research agenda for internet marketing. Presentation at UCLA (2000)
4. Kotler, P., Armstrong, G.: Marketing – An Introduction. Prentice Hall, London (1997)
5. Kotler, P.: Marketing Management – Analysis, Planning and Control. Prentice Hall, Englewood Cliffs (1972)
6. Maslow, A.: Motivation and Personality. Harper and Row, Manhattan (1954)
7. Lindskog, H.: Market segmentation based on time. Lecture at University of Linköping (2000)
8. Lindskog, H., Brege, S.: Time-rich and time-poor consumer behavior – the importance of time in market segmentation. In: Owsinski, J. (ed.) Transition and Transformation: Problems and Models. MODEST, Warsaw (2002)
9. Newman: Silicon Valley Incubator. National Geographic, December 2001
10. Robinson, P., Faris, C., Wind, Y.: Industrial Buying and Creative Marketing. Allyn & Bacon, Boston (1967)
11. Romer, P.: Time: It Really is Money. Information Week (2000)
12. Schiffman, L.G., Kanuk, L.L.: Consumer Behavior. Prentice Hall, Upper Saddle River (2000)
13. Wolfinbarger, M., Gilly, M.: Shopping Online for Freedom, Control and Fun (2000)
14. Lee, H., Whitley, E.A.: Time and Information Technology: Temporal Impacts on Individuals, Organizations, and Society. Taylor & Francis, Milton Park (2002)
15. VALS. http://www.strategicbusinessinsights.com/vals/ustypes.shtml. Accessed 14 Apr 2020
16. Donna, L.: Hoffman website Center for Connected Consumer. https://postsocial.gwu.edu/. Accessed 14 Apr 2020

Integrated System for Students' Evaluation Using KM Approach

Rabih Haddad[1,2(✉)] and Eunika Mercier-Laurent[1,2]

[1] CRESTIC Laboratory, University of Reims Champagne-Ardenne,
Reims, France
Rabih.Haddad@epita.fr
[2] EPITA Engineering School of Computer Science, Le Kremlin-Bicêtre, France
http://www.univ-reims.eu/, http://www.epita.fr/en

Abstract. With the number of international students increasing globally and the mobility of students is becoming a condition to secure a good job and to gain a shining career, evaluating candidates' prerequisites is becoming challenging. This paper presents how knowledge management approach using AI techniques could help academic institutions in the evaluation of international students' profiles by providing an adapted methodology. This methodology implemented in the proposed system will help institutions gain more time in processing students files, provide accurate evaluation of candidates by taking their cultural background into consideration and avoid human errors.

Keywords: Higher education · International students · Knowledge management · Text mining · Machine learning · Speech recognition

1 Introduction

1.1 Review

In only 10 years (2006–2016), the student population worldwide grew by almost 50%, passing from 146 million to 218 million students, representing a growth of 4.1% per year. The number of students on international mobility is rising steadily and students in the world are more and more numerous to study abroad. In 2016, almost 5.1 million of students were on the move around the world (out of 218 million) compared with only 2.9 million in 2006. The development of higher education in the world, the competition of establishments and their internationalization as well as the multiplication of agreements and equivalencies of degrees are as much factors of a rapid increase in degree seeking mobility. Thus, the massive local investment in education found in many countries contributes to the creation of regional education centres. They offer the possibility to a greater number of students from the same geographical area to access a higher education outside their country of origin and thus encourage student mobility. They set a quality higher education offer at proximity and at a lower cost. Those 5.1 million students who have crossed the borders to obtain a higher education degree, it is a symbol of the growing interconnection of higher educational systems and globalization and career opportunities. The main trends in global student mobility confirm the

© IFIP International Federation for Information Processing 2020
Published by Springer Nature Switzerland AG 2020
E. Mercier-Laurent (Ed.): AI4KM 2018, IFIP AICT 588, pp. 14–24, 2020.
https://doi.org/10.1007/978-3-030-52903-1_2

attractiveness of the English - speaking countries (United States, United Kingdom, Australia and Canada) and Europe remains the first destination for students coming from Asia (China and India in particular).

France hosts each year international students willing to pursue their higher education in different fields. Their presence compensates for the relative lack of talented French students. The state and the French educational organizations want to increase the number of students to improve the position of the French educational system vis-a-vis the Anglo-Saxon system, among others.

More than 300,000 students annually from 180 different countries got enrollment in the French Universities and Graduate Schools. These academic institutions receive thousands of applications of the students who have completed their high school, bachelor, or master's degrees. This diversity of students' profiles and their different academic background make accurate assessment an extremely challenging task. Up to now, the prior learning assessment of candidates and the processing of their applications are done manually and hence these tasks are time consuming and involve a lot of human potential errors in the selection. In addition, the distinctiveness of the French education system especially with its "Grandes Ecoles" that are unique, complicates the task of evaluation. International standard exams like SAT, GMAT, GRE are insufficient to conduct a full assessment.

In addition, being in the higher education system for the last 10 years and from personal experience I have noticed that the assessment exams that are organized by the hosting institution are not measuring the right indicators to detect the eligibility of international students to the desired higher studies programs. To me admitting relevant profiles is still an unresolved issue that should be taken into consideration. As per my knowledge and the state of the art, there is no automated intelligent system that performs a multi-criterion evaluation of international students by communicating to them. Knowing the proposed programs, computer trends and needs of students, this system should propose an adjustment of programs.

1.2   Need

What is missing? As per our knowledge existing systems lack of considering criteria such as cultural aspects, level of education in each country, motivation, real meaning of motivation letter, and emotional intelligence. In the light of the current state of the art and on our knowledge, there is no automated intelligent system that performs a multi-criterion evaluation of international students by multi-media and multi-modal interaction with them. Knowing the proposed programs, computer trends and needs of students, this system should also propose an adjustment of programs, according to the student's level. Here comes the need for automated multi-criteria system for the evaluation of students' knowledge and motivation (Fig. 1).

Many researchers and universities have worked on several systems to evaluate the students' profiles to provide coherent admission results and to process the maximum number of applications possible. One of these approaches is to compare the profiles of new applicants with those who have similar profiles and have already validated their academic programs. A second approach was based on ranking of applicants by using the available historical data and predictive analysis to detect the risk of admitting those

➤ Projected growth in international degree-seeking mobility by 2030

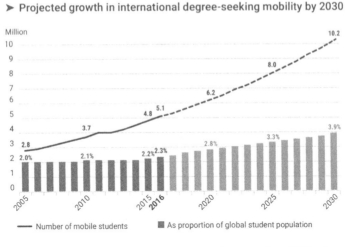

Source: Campus France projections from data from UNESCO Institute for Statistics, January 2019, based on assumed annual growth of 5.1% over the period 2017–2030.

Fig. 1. International mobility growth

candidates. Authors use these data to orient students toward a specified major or domain. In my opinion, all of these approaches do not serve to solve the main problem presented in this paper as they do not provide a subjective and adapted assessment exercises. Also, those systems do not evaluate international students' attended universities and their learning outcomes. In addition, the decision support system implemented do not use the latest technology.

1.3   Students Mobility Risks

The potential drawbacks that globalization might have on education are increasing and becoming a main worry. As mentioned earlier, the number of international students is increasing, and students' mobility is becoming a crucial phenomenon to obtain a good degree and secure a decent job. Universities have tripled their efforts to recruit and attract international students, but their educational ecosystem is still missing some fundamentals. Ensuring that all international students are admitted using an adapted admission system, receiving assistance and decent welcome from international faculty and staff, and building their career after are factors that reduce the negative impacts of globalization in education. Difficulties are summarized into 4 main categories. The first category is related to the fact that the current assessment is not adapted to the programs and hence it is measuring irrelevant indicators. The second category is that the evaluation criteria does not address the cultural aspects of candidates. The third is related to the limitation in the human capacity of treating an important number of candidates/applications over time. The last is how to reduce the impact of this mobility on education. Hence the major focus of the research is to find the automated system that addresses the 4 main difficulties already presented.

In this paper, we are going to present the related work, research methodology, challenge, and the proposed system for evaluating the students' profile using knowledge management.

2 Challenge

To remove this lock and define an effective system architecture, a deep understanding of the admission principles and related contexts is mandatory. Existing experience and explanation of the admission problem from the educative point of view must also be considered. Difficulties are summarized into 4 main categories. The first category is related to the fact that the current assessment is not adapted to the programs and hence it is measuring irrelevant indicators. The second category is that the evaluation criteria does not address the cultural aspects of candidates. The third is related to the limitation in the human capacity of treating an important number of candidates/applications over time. The last is how to reduce the impact of this mobility on education. Hence the major focus of the research is to find the automated system that addresses the 4 main difficulties presented above.

Today applying to any degree seeking program in France or anywhere in the world nationally or abroad requires that candidates should undergo an admission procedure to assess the profile of candidates and to announce the final decision (admission/refusal of candidates). Admission systems vary from one country to another and from one institution to another. The characteristics of each country and institution shape the admission system, however there is a big percentage of commonality between these systems as they require the same traditional documentation, evaluation, information: admission and languages proficiency exams, interviews, CVs, transcripts, motivation letters, and recommendations letters.

2.1 Admission Systems

In the last 10 years, most academic institutions have automated their application process and gave the international and national students the possibility to apply online to a desired program. Applying to any degree seeking program in France or anywhere in the world nationally or abroad requires that candidates should undergo an admission procedure that starts from uploading the official documents requested by each institution till the announcement of results. Admission systems vary from one country to another and from one institution to another. The characteristics of each country and institution shape the admission system, however there is a big percentage of commonality between these systems as they require the same traditional documentation, evaluation, information: admission and languages proficiency exams, interviews, CVs, transcripts, motivation letters, and recommendations letters. The admission cycle can be summarized in the below figure:. Up to now, all institutions need the candidate information and exams results to decide of the admission status of candidates. The admission procedure that is widely used worldwide and in France is described as follows (Fig. 2):

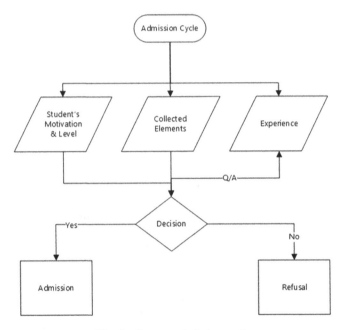

Fig. 2. Current admission cycle

- Students apply online on the institution website by supplying all the relevant and requested documents.
- Admission teams process the files following the order:
  - Relevance of the candidate to the requested major
  - Candidates high school or bachelor grades
  - Candidates experience and skills
  - Interview conduction (remote or face to face) to detect: genuineness, motivation, and capacity
  - Exams conduction to detect knowledge and practice
  - Financial status (mainly Anglo-Saxon institutions)
- Results announcements.

2.2   Knowledge Blocks

As an entry point to understanding the admission system, we should look at 2 major knowledge blocks that contribute to the relevant evaluation of students' profiles: the Curriculum Vitae (CV) and the online interview. The CV still is an important document that helps the admission committee identify important information about the candidates and provide knowledge on student's academic and career path. The online interview helps the admission committee to detect motivation and validate the coherence and genuineness of the candidates' vis-a-vis their CVs and profiles. For this purpose, the online interviews will be registered and rerun for the offline evaluation.

Curriculum Vitae (CV)

This block is very essential in the evaluation process. The amount of text that is generated every day is increasing dramatically. This tremendous volume of mostly unstructured text cannot be simply processed and perceived by computers. Therefore, efficient and effective techniques and algorithms are required to discover useful patterns. Text mining is the task of extracting meaningful information from text, which has gained significant attentions in recent years. With the rapid growth of Internet-based recruiting, there are a great number of personal resumes among recruiting systems. To gain more attention from the recruiters, most resumes are written in diverse formats, including varying font size, font colour, and table cells. However, the diversity of format is harmful to data mining, such as resume information extraction, automatic job matching, and candidates ranking. Supervised methods and rule-based methods have been proposed to extract facts from resumes, but they strongly rely on hierarchical structure information and large amounts of labelled data, which are hard to collect. Since there is no standardization in the structure of resumes, high precision in the Extraction of Information automatically from the resumes is very complicated. Resumes can be in different file types with any format without having restrictions in the domain. Many technologies have begun to fill the gap between human and computer language.

In the current systems the CV students are not taken into consideration as the evaluation logic only depends on the profiles of previous students who have succeeded a certain curriculum. Hence it depends on a comparative mechanism that might be valid for students coming from the same background but might fail for a diversified group of students. This block should provide the below information about each candidate:

- Basic: to detect the country of origin of each candidate, age and gender. The country will be a crucial factor in the adapted evaluation since a cultural impact matters here.
- Academic background: to detect the institution attended by the candidate and the highest degree obtained and the number of academic years after high school. This will help also to compile a list of academic institutions worldwide that will be ranked based on students' success after enrollment and pursuing of classes.
- Professional experience: to verify the experience and skills acquired during this experience and its relevancy to the degree obtained. This will help also to compile a list of companies worldwide that will be ranked based on students' success after enrollment and pursuing of classes.

Beside the direct knowledge that will be extracted from CVs, text mining procedures will be applied to derive knowledge from the unstructured text by merging all the above listed information. The initial work on the CV could be divided into 3 phases. The fist phase is the CV extraction. The main role of this phase is to transform any CV document to a simple text data. The recommend phase is applying natural language processing with machine learning to label the text in the CV. The last phase will be applying rules to produce a simple table where each row represent a candidate and each column represent a CV subsection. Once this table is obtained, the next step will be the evaluation of CV in context of each application by using machine learning. We will apply statistics, analytic, semantic and natural language processing algorithm and output of this exercise could be a weighted mark that aggregate CV main parts.

Online Interview

This exercise will serve in providing several types of knowledge on candidates. As per our observation and knowledge the interviews exercises for admission are crucial and are still useful today for recruitment activities, in academic or corporate affairs. They are the most important element in the admission process that universities cannot avoid despite their costs. Interviews provide necessary knowledge on candidates and their advantages are they provide a strong tool to check the social capabilities of the student under an academic ecosystem. Interviews will good elaborated questions, can manage to get valuable information on the candidate, digging deeper in the skills of the subject and the capacity to use them efficiently in the academic and corporate environment.

The online interview will be used to evaluate the English language level of candidates, their motivation, their capability to present themselves and present a coherent project of life, and some easy behavior aspects. The following 3 groups of knowledge could be extracted and evaluated from pre-registered video interviews:

- Detect the candidates' oral ability by evaluating the first couple of minutes of their interview.
- Analyze the candidates' behavior in the video in terms of self-confidence and coherence.
- Evaluate the candidates' answers to the interview questions to detect their motivation and relevance.

The 3 knowledge groups would be based on motivation, skills, professionalism, feelings and integrity. Our proposition is that motivation can be detected from audio intensity and voice security. It can also be deduced from the diversity of answers on the different questions. For the skills group, this should be evaluated based on a preselected skills set that candidates mainly possess when they are applying to similar programs. Also, a cross verification exercises against the CV results will help validation the skills acquired by candidates. Professionalism can be detected from the camera stability, face positions and orientation angles. For the feelings, presents the list of feelings that has been detected during the interview. It can be detected in the audio according to the voice parameters and characteristics and the content can be analyzed to detect if the overall opinion and usage of words is "positive" or "negative". To detect the candidate's integrity and attempts to cheat, an estimation of the gaze angle will be calculated to verify if the candidate is reading from a paper or looking outside the screen. Cheating attempt can result in a very bad grade for the candidate. For the evaluation purposes, any video will be broken down into frames and analyze each frame on its own, saving the detected characteristics in a set of results. At the end of analyzing the video, we will get a huge set that contains all the result sets from all the frames. The idea is to retrieve the audio files from the registered interviews. The following techniques could be used to have a precise evaluation: speech recognition, Large Vocabulary Continuous Speech Recognizer, Speech analytic and Semantic

Interpretation for Speech Recognition. The output of this simulator could be a weighted mark on a scale of 5 (poor, fair, good, very good, excellent for example). This mark could be an aggregate of the language, motivation, behavior, and character. There is a possibility also to convert to text to apply the text mining techniques.

3 Proposed System

3.1 Initial Architecture

The comprehension of the nature and contexts of the elements leading to the correct evaluation will guide the choice of knowledge models and processing methods. The proposed architecture will contain several communicating building blocks. Working on the algorithm requires treating a list of modules that build up the main architecture.

These modules can be in the below order:

- Exploration of the elements gathered during collection phase and comprehension of the relations in system's components. Collected elements include information found during the educational research part. Exploration should include knowledge discovery and required analysis, as well as behavioral detection. The architecture will be adapted based on the educational research results.
- Generation of an adequate exam. The exam should consider the results found in the previous research and the academic profile of each candidate.
- Generation of the GAAF (Global Admission Acceptance Factor). This is the specific measure of student knowledge and capacity, that may vary according to the requirements.

Developing the system, the nature of data, information and handled knowledge must be taken into consideration. In the case of a rich database with a lot of decision factors, BIG DATA principles and procedures could be applied (data mining, predictive analytics, double agent, analysis of user behaviour). The system (or the algorithm) should help finding the auto-adapted evaluation criteria per candidate. The Machine Learning problem will be dealt to discover the methods to be used (Random Forests, Support Vectors Machines). The challenge would be to find or build an effective system for this type of evaluation, and to implement and test it on a couple of cases. The developed system will be validated based on real cases and on the integrated feedback experience. It will be parametrized according to each institution and according to the accumulated data received during processing of new applications. After the validation of the system, we are committed to design a modular demonstrator, reusable, scalable and generic to perform the tests and get the necessary feedback on this prototype. This system is developed based on the experience accumulated in EPITA International Master's program and its student recruitment system (CRM) It is tested in this environment and could be extended for example to be part of another projects (Fig. 3).

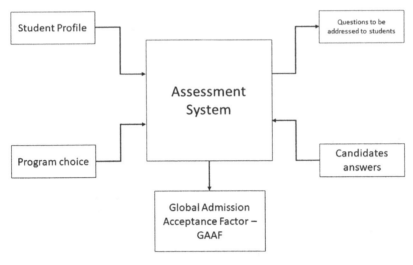

Fig. 3. System principles

3.2   Architecture

The above architecture was proposed at the beginning of the research. While starting the conception of simulators and building the model of the proposed system, this architecture has evolved and transformed into several formats. The first form was a simple decision tree that elaborate the main functions of the proposed system, as shown in Fig. 4.

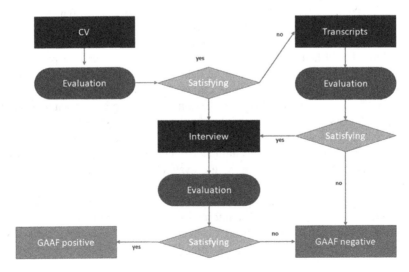

Fig. 4. Decision tree

To have a deeper vision of the decision tree, a new detailed architecture has been established that takes into account in a granular level all the aspects of the proposed system. This architecture represents a cross functional design that is composed of 8 phases and it involves all the knowledge blocks to be studied. The first phase is about receiving all the documents related to the candidate application. Those documents will be the main input of the evaluation system. They include the CV, transcripts, program choice, academic information, personal information, support letters and language records. The second phase and third phase are simply the information extraction to obtain the information model corresponding to each data type. In the fourth phase, machine learning algorithms will applied to generate the first evaluation engine for eligibility and CV assessment. The fifth phase is to simply present the result and for analyse them. In the sixth and seventh phase, deep learning algorithms will be introduced for the video behavioural analysis and video answers evaluation. The eighth and last phase will be the generation of the second evaluation system to produce the seventh results and generate the GAAF factor (Fig. 5).

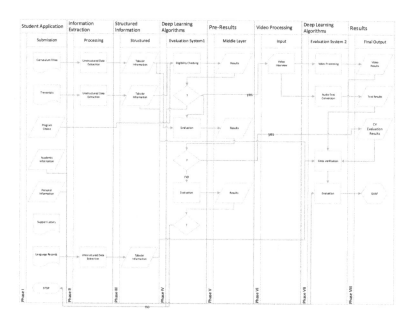

Fig. 5. Detailed architecture

4   Conclusion

In this paper, the integrated system of student's evaluation using knowledge management approach is presented. The main aim is to assess how KM can help in a such system. By presenting and analyzing the 2 major knowledge blocks that constitute the evaluation system, we will be able to obtain an architecture that leads to an adapted evaluation of candidates. Also, this analysis will help us to validate the proposed solution using real cases and integrated feedback experience. The advantage of the proposed exam is that it does not assess only the aptitude and the knowledge of the candidate in a certain domain. It goes beyond the instantaneous evaluation of students to assess the experience, the skills acquired and the behavior in a multinational environment. The next step will be building up 2 simulators based on the CV text mining block and the interview evaluation block. These 2 simulators will be tested on hundreds of students applications we own to verify their outputs and validate the proposed algorithm. These 2 simulators will be crucial to building up the architecture of the proposed system and test in real case scenarios.

References

1. Fong, S., Biuk-Aghai, R.P.: An automated university admission recommender system for secondary school students. In: ICITA 2009 (2009)
2. Nagy, H.M., Aly, W.M., Hegazy, O.F.: An educational data mining system for advising higher education students. World Acad. Sci. Eng. Technol. **7**(10), 175–179 (2013)
3. Fakeeh, K.A.: Decision Support Systems (DSS) in higher education system. Int. J. Appl. Inf. Syst. (IJAIS) (2015)
4. Vohra, R., Das, N.N.: Intelligent decision support systems for admission management in higher education institutes. IJAIS **2**, 63 (2011)
5. Hien, N.T.N., Haddawy, P.: A decision support system for evaluating international student applications. In: Frontiers in Education Conference - Global Engineering: Knowledge Without Borders, Opportunities Without Passports (2007)
6. Moedas, C.: Open Innovation, Open Science, Open to the World. European Commission, June 2015
7. http://www.diplomatie.gouv.fr/fr/photos-videos-publicationsinfographies/publications/enjeux-planetaires-cooperation-internationale/documents-destrategie-sectorielle/article/l-accueil-en-france-des-etudiants
8. Cerisier ben Guiga, M., Blanc, J.: Rapport d'information 446 du Senat, 30 juin 2005
9. Szymankiewicz, C.: Conditions d'inscription et d'accueil des étudiants étrangers dans les universités, Rapport MESR 2005-023
10. Thaung, K.S.: Advanced Information Technology in Education. AISC, p. 126. Springer, Heidelberg (2012). https://doi.org/10.1007/978-3-642-25908-1
11. Bowles, M.: Machine Learning in Python: Essential Techniques for Predictive Analysis, 31 mars 2015
12. Runkler, T.A.: Data Analytics: Models and Algorithms for Intelligent Data Analysis, 3 août 2016
13. Campus France: Key Figures, Campus France website, 3 March 2019

ICT Platform Design for SME Collaboration

Senay Sadic[1]([⊠]), Jorge Pinho de Sousa[2,3], and José Crispim[3,4]

[1] Antalya Bilim University, Antalya, Turkey
shenay@gmail.com, senay.sadic@antalya.edu.tr
[2] University of Porto, Porto, Portugal
[3] INESCTEC, Porto, Portugal
[4] University of Minho, Braga, Portugal

Abstract. Collaboration is frequently used both in literature and in practice as a sustainability and survival strategy for SMEs. In this study, we propose an ICT Platform to support SME Collaboration in discrete complex manufacturing industries. The proposed ICT Platform is defined by a conceptual platform and functional and process flows. Initially an SME network vision is set with three dimensions; sustainability, growth, and survival. And then, a Balanced Scorecard application has been performed to translate the SME network strategy to operational level ICT initiatives. Finally based on the guidance received from the literature and the established ICT initiatives, a set of ICT tools were created for the business model. These tools include a conceptual framework and the characterization of functional, informational and process flows to support the business model.

Keywords: SME collaboration · ICT platform · Process flow

1 Introduction

Small and Medium Enterprises (SMEs) represent a high percentage of the world's economic power. Forming collaborative networks is frequently addressed as a survival and sustainability tool for SMEs in the global markets [1, 2]. By joining their resources and competencies through networked manufacturing, SMEs can reach a larger dimension, access global markets, share risks, and nurture innovation through collaborative product development [3–5].

The need to align business strategy with ICT strategy and development was highlighted frequently in the literature [6, 7]. While ICT development starts from the operational level and builds through tactical and strategical levels, strategy setting starts from the strategic level and is translated to tactical and operational levels [8]. In this context, in order to develop efficient operational level ICT tools, it is therefore required to clearly translate strategic objectives into implementable operational initiatives.

In an extensive literature review, we have not come across any studies, which relate the company's business strategy with operational level ICT initiatives. Some of the reviewed papers work on the integration of the operational level, with no evidence of strategy concerns or they rather follow an incremental approach, where they initially develop business architecture and then create more focused decision support tools.

© IFIP International Federation for Information Processing 2020
Published by Springer Nature Switzerland AG 2020
E. Mercier-Laurent (Ed.): AI4KM 2018, IFIP AICT 588, pp. 25–33, 2020.
https://doi.org/10.1007/978-3-030-52903-1_3

Our main observation is that, while the theoretical literature continuously repeats the need for strategic and operational alignment and for business strategy and ICT strategy alignment, in practice and in general, applications are very limited and deceiving. On the other hand, the literature on Collaborative Networks mainly covers research to guide real life applications and focuses on developing practical tools to support inter organizational collaboration. Organizations are looking for methodologies to support a high level of integration and since collaboration brings many immediate benefits to all partners, the development of a long-term vision and of a strategy has been ignored.

In this work, we have presented the methodology that supports the design of ICT platform to support a Collaborative network. The methodology consists of three main steps: Initially the SME network vision was set as sustainability, survival, and growth. Later by implementing a balanced scorecard approach, the vision was translated into ICT initiatives, which create the base for a conceptual framework. Finally, the functional and process flows of the ICT Platform are designed and presented.

2   The Proposed Business Model

The proposed collaborative business model, designed to support SMEs functioning in discrete complex manufacturing industries, is composed of two organizational layers: SME Network and Dynamic Manufacturing Network (DMN).

While an SME network is the first organizational layer (strategic network), the DMN constitutes the second layer (operational network). SME networks are strategic partnerships of autonomous SMEs that collaborate to reach joint goals and they precede DMN formation. SME Networks provide long-term integration between network members, support their healthy operation, maintain trust and fairness between members, and develop strategies to manage the operational level decisions. The DMN, as the second layer of the business model, is defined as a temporary or long term collaborative network, that counts on joint manufacturing efforts of geographically dispersed SMEs and/or OEMs [9, 10]. DMNs are formed to satisfy specific business opportunities (either one time or repetitive) and dissolve once the orders are delivered.

Figure 1 presents the proposed business model, which functions as an intermediary between the customer and the manufacturer sides of the industry. The customer side is integrated through an e-commerce module, and a sell side marketplace is developed for customer communication.

On the manufacturing side, DMN formation and operational planning require integrated business processes and an automated, collaborative ICT platform. This collaborative platform needs to be built in order to assist the DMN life cycle, to support SME network decision making, and to monitor order processing. The collaborative platform can be used simultaneously by several DMNs that are designed to fulfill different business opportunities.

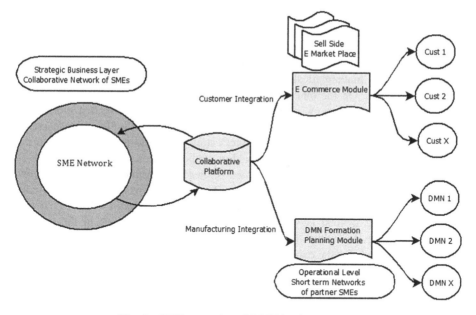

Fig. 1. SME network and DMN business model

The proposed business model requires automated processes to assist the DMN life cycle, and the business functions to support SME network decisions. A DMN works at the operational level and requires detailed focused decision support tools to enable and optimize its operations. In this context, an ICT platform should both support the back end and the front end of the whole supply chain, should facilitate interoperability among autonomous members, should enable communication flows within the network, and should assist business processes through the DMN life cycle [11].

Moreover, the development of ICT tools is necessary to decrease decision making time and increase operational efficiency. ERP applications provide control over shop floor operations but they do not provide a means to link the autonomous network members.

3   From Strategy to ICT Initiatives: A Balanced Scorecard Application

Several researchers have discussed the need for alignment of the business strategy and the ICT strategy. It is claimed that identifying a sound business strategy is the key for business process agility [6]. To successfully support business processes, the ICT strategy also needs to be aligned with the business strategy. An automated network needs to initially define its business requirements which will lead to a business architecture to be further supported by an ICT infrastructure [7]. Business model development and goal setting are clearly the basis for developing a correct information technology infrastructure.

While strategy development needs to start at the strategic level, by SME network goal setting and strategy setting, process integration needs to start at the operational level by developing a set of automated collaborative processes. In terms of process integration, as we go from bottom to top, the level of integration decreases and tools move from detailed mathematical decision support systems to conceptual frameworks or reference models. On the other hand, in terms of strategy setting, decision makers need to first decide the strategy of the SME network and later, develop ICT tools at the operational level, by translating that strategy to operational goals. In order to create successful collaborative networks, the business strategy should be integrated into the development of ICT tools and decision-making methodologies.

In order to align ICT design with business strategy, we defined the SME Network vision, and translated it into ICT strategies. The SME network vision is initially grounded on three components: sustainability, survival, and growth. While *survival* is the act of standing against economic crisis and other disturbances in the system, *sustainability* stands for withstanding internal organizational challenges. *Growth*, on the other hand, stands for the expansion of the SME network along time. This vision is then translated into operational level ICT initiatives through the Balanced Scorecard methodology.

The Balanced Scorecard (BS) framework has been widely used as a strategic management tool. Since it was proposed in the 1990s, it is has been used to measure and manage four aspects of organizational performance: Financial, Customers, Internal Business Processes, and Learning and Growth.

BS allows decision makers to extend their myopic, only financially focused-perspective, to other decision dimensions and stakeholders. In BS development, all four perspectives are guided through four major steps:

1. objectives clarify the company vision and translate it into a strategy;
2. measures provide quantitative indicators for each objective, and allow decision makers to link objectives with results;
3. targets allow decision makers to set specific goals, through long term or short term quantitative or qualitative goals;
4. initiatives recommend some actions that can be taken in order to reach identified targets for each objective

We have adapted the BS methodology by focusing on our three different vision components: sustainability; growth; and survival. We have connected each vision to one or more balanced scorecard perspective as follows: Sustainability to internal business processes perspective; growth to customers and financial perspectives; and survival to learning and improvement perspectives. Due to page limitations only sustainability balance scorecard will be presented in this section.

Table 1 presents the developed Sustainability Balanced Scorecard. In order to maintain the group cohesion and harmony required to sustain the collaborative network, the following sustainability objectives were developed: supporting conflict resolution between members; establishing high trust value, establishing high reliability value, establishing high fairness value and providing a membership management function.

Table 1. Sustainability Balanced Scorecard

SUSTAINABILITY					
	OBJECTIVES	MEASURES	TARGETS	IT INITIATIVES	ICT TOOLS
Internal Business Processes Perspective	Support Conflict Resolution between members	Visibility of Operations	none	Provide reporting for SME network decisions	**Reporting**
		Develop Initial aggrements	none	Prevent possible future conflicts by developing initial aggrements	**Membership Management**
	Establish High Trust Value within network	Trust of partners to the SME Network	max	Set and track trust measures between partners and the SME network	**Trust Management**
		Trust between partners	max	Set and track trust measures between partners	**Trust Management**
	Establish High Reliability Value	Reliability of logistics	max	Set and track reliability measures for logistics operations	**Reliability Management**
		Reliability of raw material	max	Set and track reliability measures for raw material received from suppliers	**Reliability Management**
		Reliability of the ICT Platform	none	Provide security mechanisms for the ICT Platform	**ICT Platfrom security**
		Reliability of data	max	Set and track reliability measures for the data received from partners	**Reliability Management**
	Establish High Fairness Value	Fairness of the SME Network	max	Set and track fairness measures for SME network joint functions	**Fairness Management**
		Fairness in demand sharing	none	Develop fair demand sharing mechanisms	**Demand Sharing**
		Fairness in revenue sharing	none	Develop fair revenue sharing mechanisms	**Revenue Sharing**
		Fairness in cost sharing	none	Develop fair cost sharing mechanisms	**Cost Sharing**
	Provide Membership Management	Member Profiling	none	Develop member performance Module	**Performance Management**
		Membership Management	none	Develop member association and dissociation Module	**Association Dissociation and Decision Making**

These objectives have guided us to identify the following ICT initiatives: set and track measures for each group cohesion component; provide reporting for network decisions and actions; develop pre-membership agreements; develop fair sharing mechanisms; develop member performance module; and develop a member association/dissociation DSS.

The ICT initiatives will later be classified in a conceptual framework, which will support the design of the ICT platform. A conceptual framework draws the outline for business models by defining a number of sub-models, collections of templates, procedures, methods, rules and tools.

The outputs of the Balanced Scorecards (from the previous section) have been grouped in order to create the conceptual framework. The developed framework covers three main functions: SME network support functions, e-commerce functions and DMN support functions. Due to page limitations, conceptual framework is only briefly mentioned.

4 ICT Tools

Based on the ICT initiatives, conceptual framework and literature review findings, we have developed a set of ICT tools to assist the business model. We propose here an organization of the functional flows as follows: Order Promising; DMN Life Cycle Management; Customer Relations; Membership Management; and Group Cohesion Management. Figure 2 shows the functional flows of the ICT platform and Fig. 3 presents the process flows of the system.

The overall process of operational planning in an SME network starts with a customer interaction through the e-marketplace. The production system operates under an Available to Process (ATP) strategy. Once the e-marketplace receives a new customer order, the order-promising module will be triggered, in order to check order feasibility both in terms of available capacity and required competencies. Online partner and order information will be extracted via the DMN Collaborative Platform. After the Order Acceptance submodule confirms acceptance of an order, this order will be combined with other orders for classification and prioritization.

The Order Prioritization submodule will compute order priorities, via a multi-criteria decision making tool. Order priorities will be utilized in the DMN Creation submodule, so that orders that are more valuable are processed first. On the other hand, the Order Classification submodule will compute order classes through data mining and data science approaches. Order classes can be used in strategy and promotion development for different order classes. These modules will be fed with information on order characteristics (due date, volume, processing time, etc.) and on customer characteristics.

In the DMN Creation submodule of DMN Life Cycle Management module, a multi-objective mathematical model is employed to decide DMN configuration and to compute the production and transportation lot sizes. The model will use several objectives such as cost, flexibility, partner reliability, order priority or operational risk and will take into account partner capacities, capabilities, order priorities, and costs.

The order priorities generated by the Order Prioritization submodule and customer priorities calculated by the Customer Prioritization submodule, will also be considered in the DMN formation process.

Since DMNs typically serve to a group of distinct customers, it is a good strategy to take into account customer characteristics during DMN formation. In order to enable the formation of customer and order driven DMNs, the Customer Relations module will provide its input on customer priorities and customer segments. At this stage, the

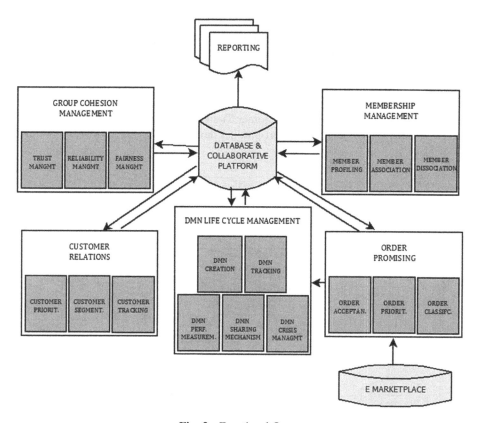

Fig. 2. Functional flows

DMN Risk Management submodule of DMN Crisis Management uses mathematical tools to predict operational risks related to DMN processes, and integrates the results to the DMN creation process. Once the DMN configuration and operational plans are set, job orders will electronically be transmitted to selected partners. In order to maintain visibility within the network, all the partners of the SME network will receive a report stating the DMN configuration and plans.

In the DMN tracking phase, if a deviation from the initial plan is detected, the DMN Event Management submodule of the DMN Crisis Management submodule will trigger an action. It may either reschedule production among current DMN partners, or include new partners to the DMN in order to assign them the failed operations. Once the operations are performed, the DMN Performance Measurement submodule assesses the performance of each partner. Moreover, DMN partners will also evaluate their trust towards the SME network and the other partners. DMN performance assessments will be stored in the Collaborative Platform database for future tracking purposes. While failing in one DMN is probably acceptable for a partner, failing frequently is an important problem that requires further attention. Finally, the DMN Sharing module will employ decision-making mechanisms to partition joint costs and benefits among partners, by taking into account their performances within the DMN.

The Customer Relations module analyzes customer data, and consists of three distinct submodules: Customer Prioritization; Customer Segmentation; and Customer Tracking. Initially, the Customer Prioritization submodule feeds the DMN Creation submodule with values for customer priorities. The Customer Segmentation submodule then creates customer segments, again based on past customer information, thus providing information that can be utilized to develop strategies and promotions for similar customers. On the other hand, the Customer Tracking submodule calculates customer preference patterns, in order to support product development.

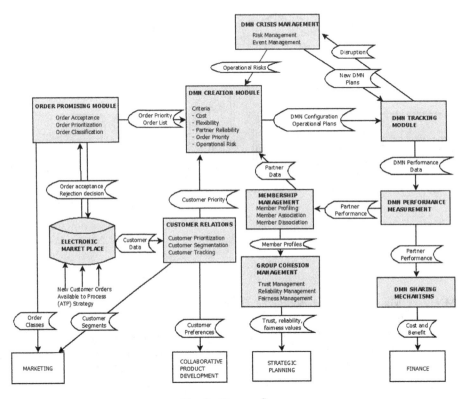

Fig. 3. Process flows

5 Conclusions

In this work, we have designed a set of ICT tools to support a business model based on two organizational layers: SME Networks and Dynamic Manufacturing Networks. Initially, we have identified three components of the SME network vision: Sustainability; Survival; and Growth. Later, we have implemented a Balanced Scorecard approach to translate the SME network vision into operational level ICT initiatives. These ICT initiatives, along with comprehensive literature review findings, provided a basis to design an ICT Platform.

Two layers of ICT Tools were designed for the business model: a conceptual framework to support SME Network functions; and functional and process flows for the business model. These instruments are expected to adequately guide the development of focused decision support tools.

Nowadays, Collaborative Networks are highly dependent on ICT platforms and automated processes. Developing such integrated tools by following a well-defined methodology will have several benefits. Since partners get involved in these collaborative networks mostly for long-term advantages, developing a long-term vision and aligning strategy with action improves the credibility of the Collaborative Network in the partners' perspective. Moreover, it broadens the short term oriented, financial benefits-focused perspective into longer-term objectives, such as growth, sustainability and survival. Developing a clear vision and implementing it into operations increases the resilience of organizations in today's turbulent markets. Moreover, automated processes working with real time data significantly shorten the decision making time and make the operational execution much easier.

References

1. Camarinha-Matos, L.M., Afsarmanesh, H., Galeano, N., Molina, A.: Collaborative networked organizations – concepts and practice in manufacturing enterprises. Comput. Ind. Eng. 57(1), 46–60 (2009)
2. Carneiro, L., Shamsuzzoha, A., Almeida, R., Azevedo, A., Fornasiero, R., Ferreira, P.S.: Reference model for collaborative manufacturing of customised products: applications in the fashion industry. Prod. Plan. Control 25, 1–21 (2013)
3. Camarinha-Matos, L.M.: Collaborative networked organizations: status and trends in manufacturing. Annu. Rev. Control 33(2), 199–208 (2009)
4. Chen, Z., Li, L.: Information support technologies of integrated production planning and control for OEM driven networked manufacturing: framework, technologies and case. J. Enterp. Inf. Manag. 26(4), 400–426 (2013)
5. Afsarmanesh, H., Camarinha-matos, L.M., Msanjila, S.S.: On management of 2nd generation Virtual Organizations Breeding Environments. Annu. Rev. Control 33, 209–219 (2009)
6. Coronado, A.E.: A framework to enhance manufacturing agility using information systems in SMEs. Ind. Manag. Data Syst. 103(5), 310–323 (2003)
7. Gunasekaran, A., Ngai, E.W.: Information systems in supply chain integration and management. Eur. J. Oper. Res. 159(2), 269–295 (2004)
8. Gunasekaran, A., Yusuf, Y.Y.: Agile manufacturing: a taxonomy of strategic and technological imperatives. Int. J. Prod. Res. 40(6), 1357–1385 (2002)
9. Markaki, O., Kokkinakos, P., Panopoulos, D., Koussouris, S., Askounis, D.: Benefits and risks in dynamic manufacturing networks. In: Emmanouilidis, C., Taisch, M., Kiritsis, D. (eds.) APMS 2012. IAICT, vol. 398, pp. 438–445. Springer, Heidelberg (2013). https://doi.org/10.1007/978-3-642-40361-3_56
10. Viswanadham, N., Gaonkar, R.S.: Partner selection and synchronized planning in dynamic manufacturing networks. IIE Trans. Robot. Autom. 19(1), 117–130 (2003)
11. Liu, J., Zhang, S., Hu, J.: A case study of an inter-enterprise workflow-supported supply chain management system. Inf. Manag. 42, 441–454 (2005)

Platform for Knowledge Society and Innovation Ecosystems

Eunika Mercier-Laurent[(✉)]

CReSTIC, University of Reims Champagne Ardenne,
France Moulin de la Housse, BP 1039, 51687 Reims Cedex 2, France
eunika.mercier-laurent@univ-reims.fr

Abstract. This paper reminds main components of Knowledge Society and of Innovation ecosystems and discusses the conditions for sustainable and successful innovation in the context of ubiquitous digitalization and third hype of artificial intelligence. It points out the necessity of having a collaborative platform for accelerating and succeed innovation. It considers the main system blocks and interactions between the components of the Innovation Ecosystems in aim understanding and maintaining the balance of knowledge-based Innovation ecosystems. The emphasis is also on early evaluation of the impacts. An architecture of artificial intelligence-based platform for collaborative gathering, sharing and exploring knowledge supporting the dynamics of the Innovation Ecosystems is presented and interaction between components discussed. We suggest applying the presented approach to European innovation ecosystem.

Environmental aspects of innovation are discussed in aim inspiring eco-design, eco-innovation, green software, circular energy and smart circular economy.

Keywords: Knowledge Society · Innovation Ecosystems · Artificial intelligence · Collaboration · Innovation process · Impacts

1   Introduction

The term of Knowledge Society has been (re)introduced over two decades ago [1–4], while Mesopotamia inspired some of the most important developments in human history, Egypt, Babylon, China, Greece, Rome, Mayas and others were Knowledge Societies. In these societies, knowledge was reserved to the elite or was open. Huge amount of past knowledge disappeared with decline, has been lost lack of knowledge transfer or simply "replaced" by new trends, due to human nature.

Today some consider that Knowledge Society involves necessarily higher education and combine research and technology in the innovation process leading to entrepreneurship and job creation [5–7].

UNESCO works to create inclusive knowledge societies and empower local communities by increasing access to, preservation, and sharing of information and knowledge in all of UNESCO's domains. Knowledge societies must build on four pillars: freedom of expression; universal access to information and knowledge; respect for cultural and linguistic diversity; and quality education for all [8]. They believe that

© IFIP International Federation for Information Processing 2020
Published by Springer Nature Switzerland AG 2020
E. Mercier-Laurent (Ed.): AI4KM 2018, IFIP AICT 588, pp. 34–47, 2020.
https://doi.org/10.1007/978-3-030-52903-1_4

universal access to information is key to building peace, sustainable economic development, and intercultural dialogue. Promoting "Open Access to Scientific Information, Open Educational Resources, Free and Open Source Software, an Open Training Platform and Open and Distance Learning allow researchers and innovators to more easily share and use data" and provide students and educators from around the world have access to knowledge and information. UNESCO contributes to international debates on internet governance, through participation in the Internet Governance Forum (IGF) and the World Summit on the Information Society (WSIS). UNESCO does not provide any platform for knowledge storing, sharing and fructifying.

The European Union (EU) in the Treaty of Lisbon makes link between three pillars: education, research and innovation necessary for facing today challenges [5]. *Open Innovation, Open Science and Opening to the World* [9] strategy is promoted via Digital Single Market [6, 10] where technology transfer and start-ups are encouraged. The Digital Single Market strategy includes all technologies such as ICT, Future Internet, nano and biotechnology, artificial intelligence including robots, IoT, 3D, virtual reality, etc. Education and training programs follow this trend.

Such a limited choice of skills to develop may lead to disappearing of basic skills and activities essential for the sustainability of the whole society ecosystems.

Emerging interest for social innovation may improve this situation.

Except the EU Cordis base [11] providing information on all research programs and results, this strategy lacks of essential environment for exploring easily all available information and knowledge to face today challenges.

The environmental concern, mostly limited today to CO_2 emission reduction, optimizing of energy and transportation as well as to water protection is a potential source of innovation and business. Several EU programs are devoted to these topics. Various initiatives in many countries may inspire other people and organizations. The European platform EIT (European Institute of Innovation and Technology) groups the research on climate, food, raw materials, energy and mobility [13].

The current pandemic of COVID19 demands finding quickly an effective solution to stop it. Solving such a problem requires worldwide collaboration between all involved actors and smart organization of all this knowledge. Emerald offer free access to related research papers [12]. Researchers working on vaccine have already taken some initiatives of such collaboration; however, a common platform for sharing the results and eco-innovating does not exist yet.

This paper presents main components of innovation ecosystems and discusses the conditions for sustainable and successful innovation in the context of knowledge society, ubiquitous digitalization and third hype of artificial intelligence. Environmental aspects of innovation are also discussed in aim inspiring eco-design and eco-innovation.

After introduction, the concept of innovation ecosystems is presented as well as some conditions for balance are given.

The described next architecture of proposed platform for Global Knowledge Society supporting the knowledge innovation ecosystems includes the most important components and the best of technology in aim accelerating the innovation process and serving all involved actors.

This article ends by concluding remarks and some perspectives of future work.

2 Main System Components of Innovation Ecosystems

Numerous definitions of Innovation Ecosystems are available in the literature [4, 6, 14, 18]. We propose to consider those presented in Fig. 1.

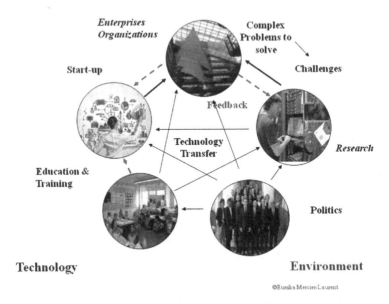

Fig. 1. Innovation Ecosystems [14]

These innovation ecosystems are composed of system elements: companies, research, government, education, technology and start-up/SME. All these elements interact and influence each other. As it represents the real situation in France and certainly other countries, some connections are one way only what affects the balance of these ecosystems and the sustainable success of innovation as well.

The innovation ecosystems interact with natural ecosystems; for example, quickly developing and changing technology use raw materials and generate waste. Planned obsolescence [15] is embedded in hardware and software as well. Exponentially increasing amount of data requires more Data Centers generating heat and cooling them is a big challenge. Few of them prototype circular energy [10, 30].

Some applications prevent human from thinking because the automated systems with embedded artificial intelligence replace human reasoning, intervention and interaction. There are also very useful applications helping people performing better their activities.

Education preparing the skills for the future has a great role to play in this context.

This model focuses on research while educational system has to explore all talents and produce all necessary skills to preserve the balance, for example cultivators, builders, service providers, etc.

A. *The Role of Education*

Education is a base of the innovation culture. While absorption of knowledge is encouraged in Europe, many skills and experiences are wasted and many are missing in the current context. There is a lack of maps and a strategy of knowledge dynamics for values creation, lack of forecast. Most of universities follow trends instead of leading. The Ministry of Education does not always accept the innovative programs proposed by some visionary beyond their time.

Web, Multimedia and ICT have provided new possibilities of "knowledge diffusion" and exchange vie e-learning, m-learning and training using various methods, including serious games, virtual reality and videos for learning gestures [19]. Many MOOCs are now available on line.

However, most of channels are mainly one way. Learning on line is complementary to live learning and give access to many. The creativity and collective intelligence that are cornerstone for innovation need more than on line knowledge absorbing.

As mentioned previously, the EU Lisbon strategy [5] considers 3 pillars: education, research & innovation.

According to Jacques Delors [32] the objectives of educational programs are learning to Know, learning to Do, learning to Live and learning to Be. These points are a part of the innovation culture. Mercier-Laurent [14] adds learning what to learn, learn to listen and understand, and learn how to solve problems using knowledge.

Developed countries are in transition from industrial era to the Knowledge Economy, which involves some essential changes. Table 1 presents some changes related to the above transition.

Table 1. Some changes induced by Knowledge Economy [14]

Industrial economy	Knowledge economy
Industrial company	Extended and learning enterprise
financial capital	Capitals: financial, intellectual, customer, patents, products, connections
Planning by project	Research of opportunities, reactivity
Risk management	Risk taking
Value of the company	Value of the connections
Work inside a company	Mobility
Processes of the company	Collaborative innovation
Training	Continuous education, e- and m-learning
"Customer-supplier" business model	New business models
Employee	Entrepreneur
Integration of environmental aspects	Environment as a source of business

This dynamic context induces the new focus and new roles, compared to industrial era. Some on them are highlighted in the Table 2. For example, the role of enterprise manager changes from planning, organizing, staffing and controlling to leader, visionary and strategist, focused on sustainable success; those of R&D manager changes from Managing R&D project to managing the eco-innovation dynamics. Manager of Human resource has to find and manage talents and Intellectual Capital [14, 25]. Financial manager focused today on ROI, has to manage organizational innovative capacity and add to ROI intangible values.

Education should also prepare for entrepreneur role. The dynamic world we live requires flexibility – for ex. Artificial intelligence evolves some professional activities and demands needs new talents.

The innovation in educational programs and training as well as detection and management of talents contribute to the balance of innovation ecosystems.

Table 2. Contrast in managerial roles [14]

Industrial economy		Knowledge economy
Functional title	Focus on	New role
Enterprise manager	Planning, organizing, staffing, leading or directing, and controlling an organization (a group of people or entities) or effort for the purpose of accomplishing a goal	Leader, visionary and strategist, focus, on dynamic governance, Sustainable success manager, stakeholders, strategic alliances
R&D	Managing research and development projects	Manager of the e-co-innovation dynamics
Human resources manager	Managing human resources, training and lay-off	Talent miner and optimizer, manager of the intellectual capital
Marketing Manager	Market study and customer relation	Opportunity hunter risk taker
Communication Manager	image	Image, links maker
Corporate social responsibility manager	Image, environmental impact, recycling, CO2 emission	e-co-innovation, minimizing the impact and packaging, nature inspired design
Project manager	Managing tasks and people, reporting	Facilitator of the collective intelligence and creativity able to motivate and valuate
Practitioner of the *faster, cheaper, better*	Manager of delocalization, cheaper workers finder	Practitioner of the e-co-innovation culture
Financial	Estimation of ROI (return on investment)	Measuring the capacity to innovate and the of tangible and intangible benefits and values
Computer user	Planning, reporting, scoring	Master of ICT (intelligent and creative technology), able to take the best technology

B. *Research Start-up and other enterprises*

The sustainable success of innovation requires two ways communication between components shown in Fig. 1, while the majority focuses only on one – pushing the research results to companies. The other way may be much more challenging for research. PhD and other researchers may find interest in challenging complex problems to solve, that can be consider at individual level or in collaborative projects, often multi-disciplinary.

In search of boosting economic growth, since several years universities in Europe has been encouraged the PhD students for transferring their research results to start-ups. Department of technology transfer offers project evaluation and links to funds. As the evaluation system does not encourage the entrepreneurship, some students prefer to continue as researchers. Star-up is risky and many afraid to fail.

Research policies, evaluation and ranking systems, synergy with companies and consideration of environmental impacts contribute all to the balance.

The well-organized and managed knowledge flow supported by right technology as a blood feed the exchanges facilitating creativity and transformation of ideas into sustainable success.

Innovation ecosystems are the cornerstone of the prosperous Knowledge Society.

C. *Role of Politics*

Government is in charge of innovation policies, of educational programs, of research policies and incentives for star-ups and small companies. They are supposed to have a vision of country development, set environmental rules, and decide taxes and regulation. They inform the targeted population about the laws, plans and principles to follow, but citizens have a very weak influence. All this activity related to innovation ecosystems requires two ways communication and integration of feedback from the involved actors.

The European Union elaborated a very complex strategy in Innovation Union, described in details in [10]. The plan contained over 30 action points and aimed to do 3 things

- make Europe into a world-class science performer
- remove obstacles to innovation like expensive patenting, market fragmentation, slow standard-setting and skills shortages
- revolutionise the way public and private sectors work together, notably through Innovation Partnerships between the European institutions, national and regional authorities and business.

Its implementation [26] evolves from experience, but still needs improvement to achieve the mentioned goals. The skills shortage mentioned above demonstrates the urgent need for the skills/competency management system [25]. Among the last actions is the implementation of the research results.

Paradoxically in the documents that applicants (researchers/SME) have to fill when applying for funding [33] implementation is mentioned, however only the research results are evaluated during the mi-term review of sponsored project. Without overall change in project evaluation for funding and review of sponsored project, the expected implementation will stay weak, because the incentive are insufficient.

The association Knowledge 4 Innovation [27] make efforts to help members of European Parliament in improving the innovation policies to achieve the stated goal.

D. *Technology*

Technology and in particular artificial intelligence approaches and techniques plays an essential role in the innovation ecosystems by supporting the whole process, presented in Fig. 2.

An application to manage the whole process can integrate a generator of ideas implemented in "box of ideas". Such a box will be certainly useful in many companies to collect ideas of employees, partners and stakeholders. In most of them only R&D department can innovate, while many interesting ideas can come from other employees and from outside.

At the university and in schools such a box may help improving the programs or/and pedagogical methods.

The collected ideas are evaluated. At least three specialists have to check technological feasibility, market and availability of skills and competencies necessary for successful transformation of selected ideas.

At the beginning of the transformation of idea into commercial product or service, it is vital to verify some constraints before doing. It avoid the productivity paradox [4]. At this stage, it is possible to use simulators to verify the factors as feasibility, existing market, competitors, return on investment in term of tangible and intangible values and

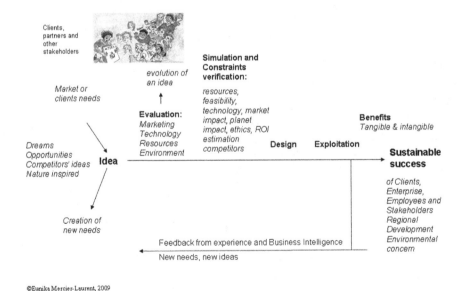

Fig. 2. Innovation process [14]

environmental impact. In the case of product simulator can help finding the best raw material and select the best design for recyclability.

E. *Environment*

All human activities generate impacts on environment. Technology, however very useful, generates a lot of waste; produces heat and affect our health. Despite numerous actions and incentives aiming in raise awareness, greedy economy and planned obsolescence reign. Greedy economy is probably among the causes of COVID19 pandemic.

The eco-design aims in integrating environmental concern via norms (ISO 26000), sometimes very heavy to apply. The partners of national sponsored project Convergence [28] developed a game to consider environmental aspects of products. EIT Platform for Innovation Community [13] includes groups working on reducing main environmental impacts.

The recent EU policy aims in protecting the environment and seeks to minimize risks to climate, human health and biodiversity. The European Green Deal aims to make Europe the world's first climate-neutral continent, in part by developing cleaner sources of energy and green technologies [29]. The emphasis is on biodiversity, climate, energy, and circular economy. The EU circular economy plan includes measures from production and consumption to waste management, and the market for secondary raw materials.

Nevertheless, the economic giants do not demonstrate their active involvement in Planet protection.

F. *Impacts*

At least seven impacts of innovation, presented in Fig. 3 should be considered and evaluated, preferably before implementation.

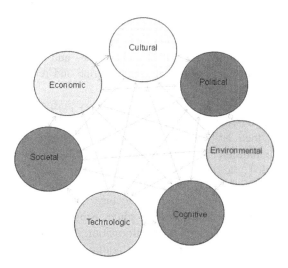

Fig. 3. Impacts of innovation [10]

The impact on **health** has to be added here, as many innovations affects directly or indirectly our health.

Generally, the reviewers of innovative projects are concerned with technological impact; sometimes with environmental and societal (Corporate Social Responsibility), but quite never with cognitive, cultural and on health. Some evaluate economic impact, but it depends strongly on professional who evaluates. Innovative project may also produce political impact in term of suggestions on improvement of innovation policies.

According to definition of Debra Amidon [4]

"Creation, evolution, exchange and application of new ideas into marketable goods and services for:

- the success of an enterprise
- the vitality of a nation's economy
- the advancement of society"

the innovation has a potential to ensure the success of the businesses, enhance the vitality of a nation's economy and bring a contribution to advancement of society. Amidon call it innovation holonomy addressing micro-, mezzo- and macro levels of society.

Innovation nourishes by knowledge. The success of innovation depends on smart organization and optimization of related internal and external knowledge (knowledge flow). Only such organization and implementation can provide the relevant and immediate access to the elements with potential to accelerate innovation.

3   Example of Platform for Global Knowledge Society

More than ever, today we have access to a plethora of various applications on servers, clouds, computers, smart phone and IoT in many fields. However, a world platform providing immediate access to relevant data, information or knowledge is still missing. This can be used for inspiration and reuse and to avoid errors as well.

There is still too much lost, forgotten or hidden knowledge. European programs have produced an extraordinary amount of technologies and solutions [34]; most of them are not easy to find with traditional search engine and remain not known. The recent results are publish in [35].

We still loose time searching, even when using very performing engines. It is not easy to find instantaneously relevant information or knowledge for various reasons. The main reason is their ad-based business model, pushing first the clients' ads. Another reason is the multiplicity of similar data and information stored in various files, applications, robots, IoT, etc.

The business model of the most of these search engines goal is not necessary finding, but transforming us into a machine to buy. The "assistants" search engine offers follow the same business rules. By consequence instead of obtaining the relevant information, these devices provide first the information about their clients that pay for the ads. Most of these assistants are not able of automatic recognition of what spoken language is used.

For all these reasons, we need effective tools for accelerating innovation.

Inspired by the by the work of Entovation network (http://entovation.com/) on Knowledge City [20] and then on Knowledge Cities, Knowledge Regions and Knowledge World [21] the Global Knowledge Society should be considered as a whole with holistic perspective and as ecosystems. During the network meeting in Helsinki 2003, the concept of En2polis [20] was born. During the next open meeting in Monterey, Mexico, this concept was extended to regions and world. Implemented latter still as concept and knowledge service [22] this movement groups representative of over 20 cities. The related association proposes annual conferences; however they do not use any platform for knowledge sharing.

Inspired by En2polis, a Platform for Knowledge society was adapted to Union for the Mediterranean (https://ufmsecretariat.org/) and presented during Global Forum 2009, Bucharest [23]. The Fig. 4 presents the system components of this platform.

It is composed of living knowledge cultivators and artificial knowledge discovery engines both influencing and preserving the environments they are a part. All platform components are connected and interact with each other. Powered by artificial intelligence and having the ability to learn, the machines (computers, smartphones, robots, etc.) would become the intelligent assistants of humans.

An ecosystem connecting users of all levels, designers of machines, software editors and researchers fueled by challenges, needs, feedback and mutual discovery of problems to be solved and technological possibilities.

The architecture of this platform is dynamic and incremental allowing adding modules that articulate with each other through reusable conceptual knowledge models

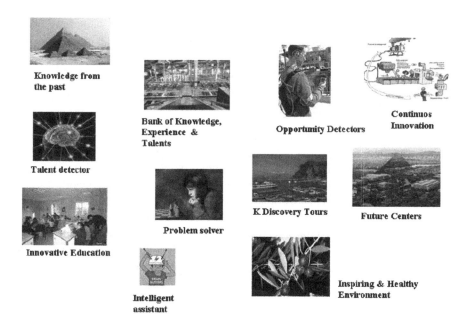

Fig. 4. Platform for Global Knowledge Society Ecosystems.

[16]. The adequate AI techniques as well as reasoning models offer a variety of efficient services including relevant search.

An appropriate education is still one of *sine qua non* conditions of a sustainable society. Innovative education at all levels, 3 W (what you want, when you want, where you want), e- and m-learning, without "walls" and borders between domains, focus on effective learning, asking right questions, connecting with right people, including the ability to apply the acquired knowledge in given situations.

Educational system includes an early detection of talents, offer measuring another IQ (imagination quotient) and various way of teaching (by playing) of global, holistic and system thinking. Such an education has the ambitious task of changing mentalities and values, of educating a culture of "knowledge cultivators', increasing imagination and creativity and taking the best from the past and inspiration from nature.

This education is based on exchanges, where we learn also to break usual connections (mental flexibility), to listen and respect, to undertake and succeed collectively; an education for all, in which technology and means of communication have a significant role to play.

Such a real time learning switches from diffusion and absorption only to listening, observing, participating, capturing, linking and opportunity hunting.

The other important points are the official recognition of new forms of organizations such as networked enterprise [4, 17] and selection of employees based on talents and not on social position.

The innovation process and in particular products design and packaging methods needs to be more nature inspired (biomimetics) [10] and produce sustainable products with embedded knowledge, which will be also used for repairing instead of recycling.

Computers and other devices must become "green", equipped with "green and intuitive software. Data center needs also optimization and adopting of circular energy principle [30].

Knowledge tours, as well as virtual and real, helps acquiring new knowledge, get a comprehension of cultural context, discovering alternative solutions or another ways of doing things and find ideas for new products and services.

Future Centers introduced by Leif Edvinsson [10] are among the places for prototyping new forms of innovation such as such as new ways of managing intellectual capital or societal innovation. However very innovative, Future Centers lack of technological platform supporting the exchanges among the members.

The European Open Innovation Strategy and Policy Group (OISPG) work in close collaboration with the European Commission. Their philosophy embraces the Open Innovation 2.0 paradigm: creation of open innovation ecosystems where the serendipity process is fully-fledged. "We believe that involving citizens directly in the innovation process allows rapid prototyping in real life. Building a prototype is the fastest, most effective way to push an idea forward. Prototyping will foster entrepreneurship in Europe, will create jobs and will boost sustainable economic and societal growth... The base our thinking on Quadruple Helix Innovation Model where government, industry, academia and civil participants work together to co-create the future and drive structural changes far beyond the scope of what any one organization or person could do alone" [31].

Except meetings, annual Yearbook [6] website [31] and group on social network they do not have a platform to accelerate innovation, share experiences and providing relevant and immediate access to their collaborative knowledge.

Our proposal of platform for them in shown in Fig. 5.

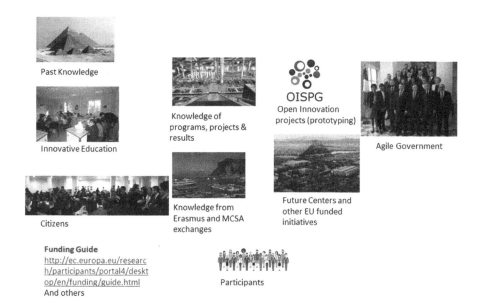

Fig. 5. Elements of platform for OISPG

4 Conclusion and Perspective

While there are many initiatives around the world on separate components of Innovation Ecosystems it will be interesting to connect them through a common platform to avoid loss of time and of energy doing similar or the same things using various lens. More collaboration on the global level may help addressing the urgent current challenges. Nevertheless, such collaboration needs an effective platform built on Knowledge Innovation principles and powered by the adequate technology.

Innovation ecosystems require organizing and optimizing knowledge for quick and relevant access. It can be done using knowledge models and combining intuitive interfaces, big data, machine learning and knowledge processing.

Overall strategy and policies should be dynamic, integrate feedback from prototyping and practice to evolve. Evaluation of impacts at the early stage of the innovation process aims in avoiding at least productivity paradox and pollution.

The future work will focus on prototyping of such a platform with incremental approach and considering environmental impact.

We also target innovation inspired by nature and centered on humans; taking advantages from past knowledge and experiences, able to make us dream, smile and live in peace, respecting each other and building a sustainable future together.

References

1. Hayek, F.A.: The use of knowledge in society. Am. Econ. Rev. XXXV **4**, 509–530 (1945)
2. Drucker, P.: The Age of Discontinuity: Guidelines to Our Changing Society. Harper & Row, New York (1969)
3. Ambrosi, A., Peugeot V., Pimienta, D.: Word Matters: Multicultural Perspectives on Information Societies, C & F edn. (2005)
4. Amidon, D.M.: The Innovation Strategy for The Knowledge Economy. Butterworth Heinemann (1997)
5. Treaty of Lisbon. Amending the Treaty on European Union and the Treaty Establishing the European Community. Official Journal of the European Union (2007)
6. "Open Innovation Yearbook" 2015, 2016, OISPG, European Union. https://ec.europa.eu/digital-single-market/en/news/open-innovation-20-yearbook-2015
7. EU group Knowledge for Innovation (K4I). http://www.knowledge4innovation.eu/
8. Building Knowledge Societies, UNESCO. https://en.unesco.org/themes/building-knowledge-societies
9. Moedas, C.: Open Innovation, Open Science, Open to the World (2015). http://europa.eu/rapid/press-release_SPEECH-15-5243_en.htm
10. Mercier-Laurent, E.: The Innovation Biosphere – Planet and Brains in Digital Era. Wiley, Hoboken (2015)
11. The EU database Cordis. http://cordis.europa.eu
12. Free content related to Coronavirus and the management of epidemics. https://www.emeraldgrouppublishing.com/promo/coronavirus.htm?fbclid=IwAR0zu1xo178fC2JFSmjA5D8iDePNzZxKotaHdMMOamS68tD_k9uRi-9lM4k
13. EIT Platform for Innovation Community. https://eit.europa.eu/who-we-are/eit-glance
14. Mercier-Laurent E.: Innovation Ecosystems. Wiley, Hoboken (2011)
15. The Battle Against Planned obsolescence. https://www.activesustainability.com/sustainable-development/battle-against-planned-obsolescence/
16. Schreiber, G., Wielinga, B., Breuker J.: A Principled Approach to Knowledge-based Systems Development. Elsevier (1993)
17. Hervé, M.: Une Nouvelle ère; sortir de la culture du chef. Ed. François Bourin (2016)
18. Russell, M.G., Huhtamäki, J., Still, K., Rubens, N., Basole, R.C.: Relational capital for shared vision in innovation ecosystems. Triple Helix **2**, 8 (2015)
19. Conruyt, N., Sébastien, V., Sébastien, O., Sébastien, D., Grosser, D.: From knowledge to sign management: a co-design methodology for biodiversity and music enhancement. In: Mercier-Laurent, E., Boulanger, D. (eds.) AI4KM 2015. IAICT, vol. 497, pp. 80–105. Springer, Cham (2016). https://doi.org/10.1007/978-3-319-55970-4_6. http://www.springer.com/gp/book/9783319559698
20. En2Polis – Knowledge City model (2003). http://www.entovation.com/group-alliance/en2polis.htm
21. "Knowledge Cities, Knowledge Regions, Knowledge World", III Roundtable, Entovation Group/Alliance and International Forum. El Tech, Monterrey, México, 1–4 November 2004. http://www.knowledgesystems.org/res_p_int_conferencias.html
22. Carrillo F.J. (ed.) Knowledge Cities. Butterworth-Heinemann (2006). ISBN 978-0-7506-7941-1
23. Mercier-Laurent, E.: Virtual Knowledge Space for UFM an amplifier of a sustainable innovation @ the speed of thought. Global Forum (2009). http://globalforum.items-int.com/global-forums/global-forum-2009-ict-the-future-of-internet-bucharest-romania/

24. Mercier-Laurent, E.: Managing intellectual capital in knowledge economy. In: Mercier-Laurent, E., Owoc, M.L., Boulanger, D. (eds.) AI4KM 2014. IAICT, vol. 469, pp. 165–179. Springer, Cham (2015). https://doi.org/10.1007/978-3-319-28868-0_10

25. Mercier-Laurent, E.: Trends and challenges for intellectual capital, chapter in intellectual capital in organizations. In: Ordonez de Pablos, P., Edvinsson, L. (eds.) Nonfinancial Reports and Accounts. Routledge, pp. 297–306 (2015)

26. European Union Research and Innovation Strategy. https://ec.europa.eu/info/research-and-innovation/strategy_en

27. Knowledge for Innovation. https://www.knowledge4innovation.eu/

28. Feng, Z., et al.: Toward a systemic navigation framework to integrate sustainable development into the company. J. Cleaner Prod. **54**, 199–214 (2013)

29. European Green Deal. https://ec.europa.eu/info/energy-climate-change-environment_en

30. Kayakutlu, G., Mercier-Laurent, E.: Intelligence in Energy. Elsevier (2017

31. OISPG. https://ec.europa.eu/digital-single-market/en/open-innovation-strategy-and-policy-group

32. Delors, J.: Learning - The Treasure Within. The UNESCO Publishing (1998). http://unesdoc.unesco.org/images/0010/001095/109590eo.pdf

33. The EU H2020 program. https://ec.europa.eu/info/funding-tenders/opportunities

34. Research*eu. https://cordis.europa.eu/research-eu/en

35. Cordis Results Pack. https://cordis.europa.eu/results-packs/en

Measuring Successful Digital Services by Identifying Active Users

Sarwar Jahan Morshed[1(✉)], Juwel Rana[1,2], and Marcelo Milrad[1]

[1] Department of Computer Science and Media Technology,
Linnaeus University, Vaxjo, Sweden
{sarwar.morshed,juwel.rana,marcelo.milrad}@lnu.se
[2] Telenor Group, Oslo, Norway
juwel.rana@telenor.com

Abstract. This paper is an extended version of the work published in [1]. We extended our previous work by the proposed model representation and more experimental result. Almost every service in the current era are either managed or operated with the help of digital services to manage their customer's activities. So digital service providers are engaging in different ways with the users to know their feedback about the service. Traditional methods for understanding user satisfaction from their direct feedback or survey. Both of these methods might produce biased result due the limited user participations. Therefore, knowledge management of user activities with the digital service could be an alternative approach for identifying satisfied users. In the previous work [1], we have presented a data science model. In this paper, more result using the proposed data science model have been presented to prove that the proposed model is workable to measure successful digital services.

Keywords: User feedback · Digital service · User satisfaction · Data science · Prediction model · Knowledge management · Service evaluation · Machine-learning algorithm

1 Introduction

There is an increasing demand for evolving digital mobile services around the world to facilitate human life and activities. Technology-based startup companies are pioneers in forming digital services in all over of the world. One of the key issues of current businesses is not only to recognize who the customers are – rather to understand users' contextual information such as their location, real-time activities and ways of communication and interaction with the different services. If the organizations do have relevant customer (of their services/products) information and behavior patterns, it will help them in making better decisions regarding the product or service development. The success of the digital services is represented by an increasing number of loyal customers. On the other hand, the loyalty of users relies on how they utilize and like the features provided by a digital service. However, understanding the powerful features as well as the digital services that are liked by a user is a challenging issue. Besides, users' behaviors are changing continuously along with the rapid moving of the digital age.

© IFIP International Federation for Information Processing 2020
Published by Springer Nature Switzerland AG 2020
E. Mercier-Laurent (Ed.): AI4KM 2018, IFIP AICT 588, pp. 48–64, 2020.
https://doi.org/10.1007/978-3-030-52903-1_5

Therefore, it is required to analysis user activities related to the digital service in order to understand the motivation or level of interests towards it (i.e. how often the user access this service, how the user the service per day, week or month) [2].

It has been a common trend to identify user's gratification with the digital services by getting the users' direct feedback on the determinants of the user satisfaction. In general, user's feedback is collected using any of the traditional forms like filling feedback forms, conducting surveys, oral questionnaires carried out by the survey team, or by getting a rating from the user after using a specific service or the product. In the age of a nomadic lifestyle, all users do not have such patience or time to give these kinds of feedback. Besides, a small number of users usually participate in these forms of feedback. Therefore, a decision based on this feedback may lead to developing the service to a wrong direction. In contrast, users of the different digital mobile services generate a large volume of user activity data that can be used to measure user's satisfaction instead of relying only on user's direct feedback data.

Analyzing such large amount of data using statistical models is difficult. Besides, current businesses require instant analysis of user feedback - which is not possible using the conventional manner of statistical analysis. In this case, appropriate Machine Learning algorithms can be used to analyze data in real time. To the best of our knowledge, there are very few proposals that use activity data to find user satisfaction. Given these circumstances, we are exploring how to develop a data science model that could be able to measure the success of a digital mobile service. The proposed model exploits user's activity data rather than user's direct feedback data for identifying his/her level of satisfaction. Thus, the main contributions of this paper can be enumerated as follows:

- We develop an innovative data science model for discovering satisfied users from digital mobile service unlabeled access login data.
- We demonstrate that the volume of the dataset is not the main pre-requisite for building such a predictive model.
- We observe that satisfied users are the key indicator for measuring the success of a digital mobile service.

The remaining of the paper is structure as follows: in Sect. 2, related research efforts are described. Section 3 illustrates the methodology and method of the proposed user satisfaction model. Section 4 depicts the experimental results based on a sample dataset used in the proposed user satisfaction model and shows that the proposed user satisfaction model could resolve the research problem mentioned in Sect. 3.3. Finally, future efforts and conclusions are presented and discussed in Sect. 5.

2   Related Efforts

Several interesting proposals for discovering the level of user satisfaction have been presented in the last couple of years [3–5]. Almost all of them worked with data science models based on the user direct feedback data. Proynova and Paech [6] identified the factors that influence user satisfaction. Nourikhah and Kazem Akbari [7] present the impact of service quality on user satisfaction. They present a model estimating the distribution of quality of experience using Bayesian data analysis, Electronic Commerce Research and Applications. These authors present a method that correlates Quality of Experience (QoE) and Quality of Services (QoS). In their approach, they use opinion score distribution instead of the mean opinion score. Besides, they use Bayesian data analysis instead of linear regression as they find two shortcomings of linear regression: (i) linear regression assumes that dependent variable complies with the Gaussian distribution and that the predictor variables are independent. (ii) The dataset used in linear regression should be metric, while other forms of data cannot be used. Their approach depends on the user feedback on QoE using which they develop their model to find the user satisfaction on QoS. Kiseleva et al., [8] proposed a model that could predict user satisfaction by using the interactive dialogue with the intelligent systems like Microsoft's Cortana, Google Now, and Apple's Siri. Kim et al., [9] present in their paper which and how variables should be considered in the data science model for user satisfaction. The authors present a forecast model for the user satisfaction on searches using the clicking data (dwell time) on the link. Hsieh and Tang [10] presents an approach to use Neural Network in meteorology and oceanography. The authors show how to use different statistical methods by improving and modifying various parameters to adjust to the problem Noh et al., [11] present the influential factors for digital home services. O'Leary [17] analyses the prediction market where he indicates that there are limited works, based on user centric data. He outlines that user centric data could provide more effective and transparent pattern of market prediction. Although most of these techniques use the users' direct feedback data, they could impact other methods on identifying the factors for measuring the level of satisfaction with the different digital services.

3 Methodology and Proposed Model

The deductive reasoning method [12] has been selected to guide and carry out our research efforts. It is a common understanding that if a user interacts with the service frequently than the average interaction (by all users) - we can claim that the user is satisfied with it. On the other hand, if the number of satisfied users is higher, it can be said that the service has a success factor. Therefore, the proposed model first estimates the satisfied users of the service by descriptive statistical analysis. Then, the user with this statistical estimation will be measured using the machine learning data science model. In this section, we present a data science model which facilitates an interpretable, multi-granular analysis of the decision-making process. We begin by discussing the problem setting and relevant details, then dive into the details of modelling and inference.

3.1   Definition of a Satisfied User

Three issues affect the level of satisfaction of a digital service user according to [13]:

- Impact of the service to the user (this impact may be social, personal, professional, or financial).
- The opportunity provided by the service. For example, social ties through the service (e.g., like, sharing contents, status update, etc.) may lead the increasing customer satisfaction.
- Usability of the service (e.g. technical difficulties are faced by the user).

All of these issues can only be measured by empirical studies (survey, questionnaire, rating, etc.). Besides, there is no benchmark value for satisfaction. Therefore, we rely on Trait theory to identified and define a satisfied user. Trait theory posits that a person's behavior will be generated consistently with his or her personality traits. There were empirical studies [15, 16] reported that personality traits have a significant relationship with customer-oriented behavior. Consumer's attitude, behavior, and thoughts are reflected through the service/product that is being used by them. They also consider these services as the brand. When a user considers and recognizes a product or service as a brand, he/she becomes active to the service/product that means that active user is an indicator of the happy user. So, from different researchers' point of view, a satisfied user means a loyal user who repeatedly uses the service or the product.

3.2   Success of the Digital Service

Customer loyalty is vital to the success of business organizations. The success of a digital service relies on the user satisfaction, while higher satisfaction makes a user loyal to a digital service. Chen et al., [18] present and analyze the factors that affect the success of a digital service. These factors are revenue efficiency, distribution model, the competition of product, service/implement model, strategic alliance, and market segment. These authors illustrated domain specific business factors rather than common factors for all IT based business or services in this paper. Therefore, these factors cannot be used to develop a generic predicting model that could measure the success of a digital service. But how can these success factors be measured? The determinants that lead most to measure the success of the digital service are (i) number of users and (ii) revenue earning [19]. These two determinants of success are influenced by the user level of satisfaction, which relies on the quality of the service. Popular services and products become brand while increasing its number of users. Considering the definition of the quality of any digital service, user happiness and benchmark of the success of the digital service, we assume that there is a hierarchical relationship among the quality of the service, the user happiness and success of that digital service – which can be presented as the Fig. 1.

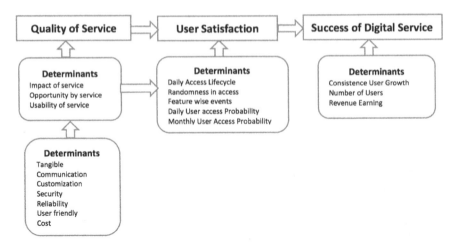

Fig. 1. Relation between user satisfaction and success of digital services

3.3   Formalization of the Problem and Research Question

Consider a decision space S holding m number of users of a digital service. There are p number of features provided by the service (i.e. the decision space is p dimensional). S contains N number of multivariate observations $\{x_1, x_2, ..., x_n\}$ interacting by the users with different features of the given service. We consider that these observations are sampled from a normal distribution. A hyperplane (decision boundary) l is required to be identified to separate the solution S' space for classifying the users into two solution space: S'_h *(satisfied)* and S'_u *(unsatisfied)*. Based on the above problem and the discussions provided in the previous sections we formulate our main research question as follows:

How to measure user's satisfaction of a digital mobile service by analyzing access service log data?

3.4   Data Description

In our experiment, event-based access log datasets are used. The dataset contains 10 million of events for 21 attributes. These datasets contain timestamp which indicates when an event has been occurred. An event is generated if a user successful login, successful authorization and so on has taken place. That means the dataset is limited within the service access authorization, however it neither contain any demographic data nor service featuring data such as feature viewed or clicked. If a particular access event is generated, '1' is assigned to the relevant attribute of that event, if not then '0' is assigned to the feature for that event. The experimental dataset contains 18 such events-oriented attributes among the 21 attributes. It is notable that these attributes cannot be used directly for recognizing the user satisfaction pattern. Therefore, we derive four features from these 18 attributes through a feature engineering mechanism. Later theses derived features have been used as predictors for estimating user satisfaction.

3.5 Data Science Model Description

Figure 2 presents the block diagram of the proposed data science model. Having our research problem defined, our proposed model uses Binary classification, since the solution space is to divide into two classes (satisfied and unsatisfied) by a decision boundary. The supervised learning model is used to train the classifier. In this case, a learning algorithm is provided a set of N labeled training examples $s\{(u_i, c_i) : i = 1, ..., N\}$ from which it must produce a classification function $f: U \rightarrow C$ that maps target variables (here users) to classes. Here u_i denotes the ith training user and ci is the corresponding classes [20]. In our given research problem, the data is not a labeled data; instead, it used unlabeled data. Therefore, the proposed model is required to develop a labeled training dataset from the given unlabeled data. Training the proposed data science model using the training dataset and discover on the test dataset are carried out in the following three stages:

- Latent variables (predictors) derivation
- Label Estimation on training dataset
- Prediction Model

Latent Variables Derivation

This stage is applied on both the training dataset and test (new) dataset. It is hard to find a pattern of the user behavior from the access log data if the dataset is unlabeled. Especially, if the user generates the observations in the sample dataset as events and the value of those events are presented in binary form. Therefore, a data science model is required to identify the unobservable variables that are used as the predictor in the data science model. The steps below are followed in order to identify the predictor variables.

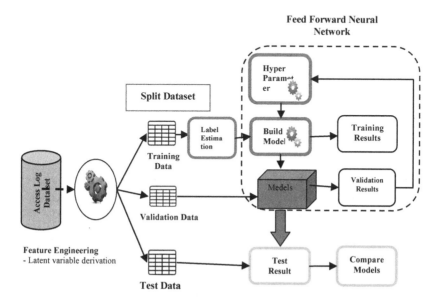

Fig. 2. Proposed data science model

Input: Experimental dataset is an unlabeled dataset F that consists of both binary data and categorical data. It is converted into a data frame (we use matrix notation to represent the data frame, as it is common to represent a spreadsheet or a tabular data frame of q rows and r columns as a matrix [21]), where q is the number of observations, and r is the number of features provided by the digital service. $f_{i,j}$ is any value (either 1 or 0, since we are using access log data) representing an event related to any feature of an individual user. Bellow we describe the steps used to derive the latent variables.

$$
F = \begin{bmatrix} f_{1,1} & f_{1,2} & \cdots & f_{1,r} \\ f_{2,1} & f_{2,2} & \cdots & f_{2,r} \\ \cdots & \cdots & \cdots & \cdots \\ f_{q,1} & f_{q,2} & \cdots & f_{q,r} \end{bmatrix} \text{ and } X = \begin{bmatrix} x_{1,1} & x_{1,2} & \cdots & x_{1,q} \\ x_{2,1} & x_{2,2} & \cdots & x_{2,q} \\ \cdots & \cdots & \cdots & \cdots \\ x_{p,1} & x_{p,2} & \cdots & x_{p,q} \end{bmatrix}
$$

Derivation of Predictors: From the dataset F, find the following latent/unobservable variables for each user and store into any data frame X that contains the derived predictors of p users and q (in this case, q = 4 as we assumed four predictors that are highly correlated derived features from our experimental dataset) is the number of derived feature. In this approach of happy user identification, we derive four different latent variables (predictors) from the raw users' access log dataset such as i) Slot wise Average Spent Time ii) Daily Interaction iii) Day wise Life cycle and iv) Feature Wise Interaction Ratio. Methods to derive these four predictors have been explained in the following. These methods are influenced by the work of Rana et al., [15]:

Slot Wise Average Spent Time, $IR_{slotwise}$: We divided the 24 h into four timeslots 00:00 to 06:00, 06:01 to 12:00, 12:01 to 18:00 and 18:01 to 23:59 to identify individual user's access pattern on a daily basis. Slot wise Average Spent Time f_s means the summation of the individual user's total events in each slot and total number of events of all user of the similar slot.

$$
f_s = \frac{\sum\limits_{i=1}^{N} \sum\limits_{j}^{s_u} e_{i,j}}{\sum\limits_{p=1}^{N} \sum\limits_{q=1}^{m} \sum\limits_{r}^{s} e_{p,q,r}}
\tag{1}
$$

Where N is the number of days in the dataset, s_u is the number of slots of user $\underline{u}$, m is the total number of users in the dataset.

Daily Average Interaction IR_{Daily}: IR_{Daily} is the individual user's daily average events (i.e. daily interaction ratio) generation and can be calculated as dividing the daily events (generated by individual user in each day) by the total events per day generated by all users.

$$
f_{di} = \frac{\sum\limits_{i=1}^{F_{md}} e_i}{d_l - d_f}
\tag{2}
$$

$e \rightarrow$ events or observation in the dataset
$F_{ind} \rightarrow$ Total number of individual events in the dataset
$d_f \rightarrow$ Individual user's first day
$d_l \rightarrow$ Individual user's last day

Day Wise Lifecycle, $Lifecycle_{Daywise}$: It means the average difference between the individual user's first access and the last access in the day.

$$f_{lifecycle} = \frac{\sum_{i=1}^{N_u} \left(t_i - t_{f_i} \right)_i}{N_u} \tag{3}$$

Where,

$t_l \rightarrow$ last access of a user in the service
$t_f \rightarrow$ first access of a user in the service
$N_u \rightarrow$ total number of days accessing the service of a user

Feature Wise Ratio, $IR_{Featurewise}$: It means the summation of the average ratio of individual user's number of events divided by the total number of events generated for a specific feature.

$$f_f = \frac{\sum_{i=1}^{F_{ind}} e_i}{\sum_{j=1}^{m} \sum_{k=1}^{F} e_{j,k}} \tag{4}$$

Where $F_{ind} \rightarrow$ *individual user's feature wise event*

Normalization of Predictors: To scale the derived features, this model normalizes the derived predictors and transform the normalized values into another data frame $\lfloor \hat{x}$. Feature scaling is used to normalize the values of each derived predictor variable between 0 and 1. Following the feature scaling formula [21] is used in this regard:

$$\hat{x} = \frac{x_{i,j} - x_{min}}{x_{max} - x_{min}} \tag{5}$$

The resultant data frame $\lfloor \hat{x}$ contains the normalized values of the predictors (as shown in the following):

$$\hat{x} = \begin{bmatrix} \hat{x}_{1,1} & \hat{x}_{1,2} & \cdots & \hat{x}_{1,N} \\ \hat{x}_{2,1} & \hat{x}_{2,2} & \cdots & \hat{x}_{2,N} \\ \cdots & \cdots & \cdots & \cdots \\ \hat{x}_{m,1} & \hat{x}_{m,2} & \cdots & \hat{x}_{m,N} \end{bmatrix}$$

If this derived data frame $\hat{x}$ is generated from the train dataset, it is used as the input for label estimation to train the prediction model. In contrast, if $\hat{x}$ derived from the test dataset, it is used as the input in the prediction model to classify the target variables.

Label Estimation on Training Dataset

This step is applied only on the training dataset since the classification algorithms require a labelled dataset as the input with the target (class) variable column to train the prediction model. We used the following label estimation function:

$$h(x) = \sum_{i=1}^{F} W_i x + b \tag{6}$$

Where x is the feature matrix, $h(x)$ is the label vector, F is the number of features, W is the weight matrix, and b is the noise. It is notable that weight and noise are randomly generated values by pre-defined function. The estimated label for training the dataset is calculated using the following conditions:

$y = 1$ if

$$h(x) \cdot \text{mean}() - h(x) \cdot \text{var}() \le h \ge h(x) \cdot \text{mean}()$$

And $y = 0$ otherwise.

Finally, we get the training dataset as follows and it consists of the latent variables. This dataset is used for training the model.

$$d = \begin{bmatrix} \hat{x}_{1,1} & \hat{x}_{1,2} & \cdots & \hat{x}_{1,N} & y_1 \\ \hat{x}_{2,1} & \hat{x}_{2,2} & \cdots & \hat{x}_{2,N} & y_2 \\ \cdots & \cdots & \cdots & \cdots & \cdots \\ \hat{x}_{m,1} & \hat{x}_{m,2} & \cdots & \hat{x}_{m,N} & y_m \end{bmatrix}$$

Prediction Model of a Satisfied User

To predict a satisfied user, we have method a Feed Forward Deep Neural Network (FFDNN) algorithm. This proposed method is influenced by a paper of Andrew Ng [22]. The model contains *four* hidden layers and each of these layers contains a weight matrix W of the input feature and a bias vector b. We compute vector h_1 which is the input layer and first activation layer of the proposed model.

$$h_1(x) = \sigma\left(W_1^T x + b_1\right) \tag{7}$$

where x is input vector that represents correlated $k \times k$ features, W_1 is the weight matrix for input layer and b_1 is the bias vectors for the first hidden layer. W can be pre-initialized or randomly generated by a customized function. In order to train our model, we use a pre-defined function that initializes the value of W. The number of neurons in each layer is considered as the bias b. For all other intermediate hidden layers, vector h_i can be defined as;

$$h_i(x) = \sigma\left(W_i^T x + b_i\right) \tag{8}$$

In this equation each column of the matrix W_i corresponds to the weights of ith hidden layer for a specific timestamp T. In all of these hidden layers, we use a non-linearity function $f(z)$ for computing the hidden layers. In our experimental implementation, the FFDNN which consists of input layer, 3 hidden layers, output layers with 350 neurons, 26401 parameters have been used. As shown in the Fig. 3, five derived features from our dataset are used in the input layer as the input neurons and outputs 200 neurons. These 200 neurons are used in the first hidden layer to produce 100 neurons which feeds into second hidden layer as input. Third hidden layer contains 50 neurons which produce the output neuron.

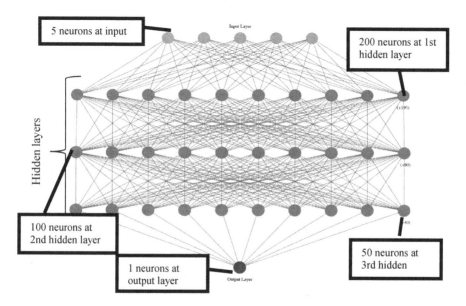

Fig. 3. Neurons in the proposed Feed Forward Neural Network

Parameters in DNN are generated by the formula below:

Parameters = *input values * neurons in the first layer + bias values*

In the first layer 1200 parameters (5 * 200 + 200). Similarly, 20,100 in the second layer, 5050 parameters in the third layer and the output layers contains 51 parameters. In our model, we utilize the Rectifier Linear Unit (ReLU) as the activation function for all of the hidden layers except the output layers. The reason behind using ReLU in our model is to get better performance for active user prediction. Rectifier is an activation function which is defined with the positive argument of this function and can be shown as in Eq. (9).

$$\sigma(z) = \max(0, z) \tag{9}$$

Where z $\rightarrow$ is the input to a neuron.

On the other hand, we have used sigmoid as the activation function in the output hidden layer as sigmoid function takes real values from the previous hidden layer and output any value of either 0 or 1. A Sigmoid function can be defined as:

$$S(z) = \frac{1}{1 + e^{-z}} \tag{10}$$

We use the sigmoid function for the following reasons:

i) Non-linear relationship between the input
ii) convert the input into a more useful output (in our case, between 0 and 1)

Again, we use the optimizer function Adam (Adaptive moment of estimation) [23]. It is a stochastic gradient method. Since Adam does not need any stationary objective f (x) might change with respect to time and still the algorithm will maintain converge. The output hidden layer takes input fifty neurons which produced from the third layer. It provides the predicted value of the label for each user. We used different epochs with 10 batch-size for training the model. We have used 'binary cross entropy as loss function' (in the proposed DNN model) as it measures the performance of a classification algorithm whose number of output is a probability value between 0 and 1. The last layer will provide an output vector y which is the probability distribution over the N output classes.

4   Experimental Results

In order to validate our concept, we have implemented the proposed model. Our experimental user access log dataset size was of 10704949 observations with 21 features. Features in this dataset are binary and timestamp. We divided the raw dataset into two before any data pre-processing: 1st 5000000 observations were used for the trained dataset and the remaining 5704949 observations for the test dataset. The first 5 000 000 observations were divided into 70%:30% ratio for training and evaluation respectively during training the model. Then, the trained model is stored to evaluate the performance of the model with the test dataset. In our experimental settings we simulate with four popular optimization algorithm such as Adam, SGD, RMSprop and Adagrad. Since any artificial neural network can defined as a stochastic process, we need to tune the hyper parameters of the optimization algorithms.

We know that value of hyper parameters varies from model to model. Therefore, we need to tune these hyper parameters during training the model to find the optimal trained model. Although, each of this optimization algorithms have different set of hyper parameters, learning rate and learning rate decay are two common parameters. We simulate the proposed model by tuning these two parameters with different values to see the impact of the accuracy of the model. We find the highest accuracy by considering the learning rate 0.005, 0.01, 0.001, 0.01 for adam, SGD, RMSpprop and Adagrad respectively. We did not find significant variation in the accuracy for learning rate decay. Therefore, we kept the value of decay 0.0 for all of these optimization algorithms. The simulated results of our experiments are shown in Table 1. The result of accuracy and RMSE in Table 1 shows that the Adam optimization algorithms provides better optimized result. In the following sub-sections, we discuss the salient result we found after analyzing this experiment.

Table 1. Accuracy and RMSE for different optimization algorithms

	Accuracy on validation dataset	Accuracy on test dataset	RMSE on validation dataset	RMSE on test dataset	Last epoch
Adam	0.8837209302	0.7837837837	0.273	0.465	194
SGD	0.5639534883	0.1756756756	0.508	0.908	1
RMSprop	0.7674418604	0.6756756756	0.404	0.569	181
Adagrad	0.7965116279	0.6351351351	0.400	0.604	193

4.1   Result Analysis and Discussion

As we know that performance of any data science model depends on three issues: i) setting the optimal model parameters ii) accuracy and error of the model and iii) how do the model produce result on dataset for particular decision making. The goal to train a model is to set the model parameters that have low loss. If the value of loss for both training data set and test dataset are consistent after certain iterations, model parameters are considered of that iteration. On the other hand, value of accuracy of a model indicates how the model performs. Besides. Value of AUC curve indicates how the model predicts correctly.

We have iterated the model 200 times to train it. From the simulation, we find that the model learns until 194 epochs when optimization algorithm is 'adam'. This indicates that the proposed model learns consistently. Based on the ''adam' optimization algorithm, the experimental result shows that the RMSE is 0.273 with evaluation data set while 0.465 with test dataset. Besides, we get 88% accuracy with validation data while 78% with test dataset. Figure 4, presents the accuracy for the given train dataset and test dataset. In the case of neural networks, the loss is negative log-likelihood. The model becomes better when loss becomes lower. Besides, the value of loss refers to how good or poor the model performs after each or a several number of epochs (iterations). Figure 5 shows that loss is decreasing as the Fig. 4 shows that the accuracy is increasing, since accuracy is inversely proportional to the loss of any model with respect to the iteration. From both of these figures, we find that the accuracy and loss does not vary significantly after 100 iterations. This indicates the generalization of the proposed model.

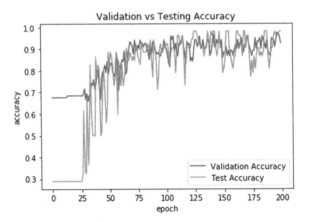

Fig. 4. Summarize history for accuracy

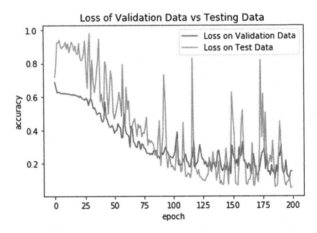

Fig. 5. Summarize history for loss

We also evaluate the model using the ROC curve. We find that the AUC score is 0.96 in the evaluation data as shown in the Fig. 6. High AUC ROC score indicates the classifier currently can perform the classification correctly. However, it requires to search the threshold for which it can classify more better. On the other hand, low AUC ROC score indicates that indicates the classifier currently cannot perform classification correctly, and even fitting a threshold will not improve its performance. In this case, our proposed model could predict an active and satisfied user correctly, as we found the AUC score in test data set is 0.93 (Fig. 7):

We also evaluated the model by varying the number of predictors. We found that a significant number of users have a very low interaction with the service. As a result, it significantly deviates the overall accuracy, precision and AUC. Therefore, we filtered out the users those who have interactions less than the mean of total users' interactions. This improves the accuracy as well as the AUC of the model.

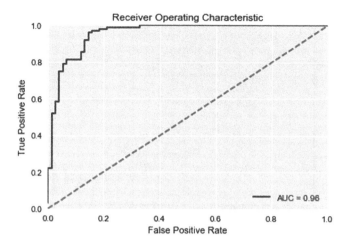

Fig. 6. ROC curve on validation dataset

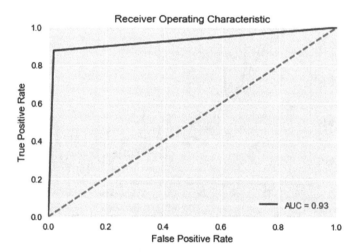

Fig. 7. ROC curve on test dataset

Figure 8 shows the decreasing mean absolute error and finally the value becomes around 0.1 which indicates the proposed model would predict accurately. As we know that the MSE indicates the difference between the predicted value and targeted value. Figure 9 shows that the model very small mean squared error that shows the correctness of the model.

Besides, all predictors that we have derived from the raw dataset are slot wise interaction in each day, daily interaction, feature wise interaction, and user's Lifecyle in each day in the system. Our experiment shows that all of these features are highly correlated to measure user's activeness in the digital system. Therefore, we can argue that if someone spend a countable time regularly with the digital mobile service, one can be a satisfied user.

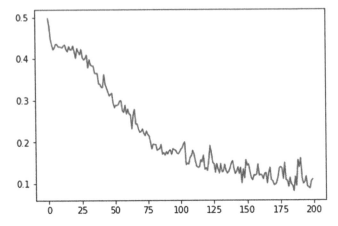

Fig. 8. Summarize history of Mean Absolute error

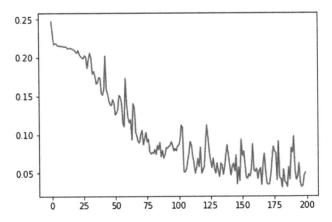

Fig. 9. Summarize history of mean squared error

5 Conclusion

In this extended version of the paper of [1], we present a data science model to discover satisfied users of a digital mobile service. The novelty of this approach is that it uses the user's access log data of the given service rather than user's direct feedback data. Knowledge Management paradigm is used during designing the proposed data science model. We show that the model is able to classify users as satisfied and un satisfied. We also evaluate the performance of the model using performance matrices such as accuracy, and ROC-AUC curve. The accuracy scores derived using these matrices above 90% for both validation and test dataset – which indicates a good and acceptable value for a data science model. We use a dataset of 10 million of user observations (events) in our investigation for the proof of concept of the proposed model. This proposed model shows that any size of dataset can be used to develop a promising prediction model using a Deep Neural Network. In this way, we also show that active and satisfied users can measure the success of digital service, if we could classify them. Besides, a large scale of user access log dataset can be used to see the performance of the proposed model, and we left open this task of scalability of the model as the future work. We have been also working with other users access log dataset to see how this proposed neural network model works.

References

1. Sarwar, J.M., Juwel, R., Marcelo, M.: Active and satisfied users as a key to measure the success of a digital mobile service, AI-based innovation in digital services. In: Proceedings of 6th AI4KM, 15 July 2018, Stockholm (2018)
2. Top 12 Key Performance Indicators for Maximizing Mobile App Revenue, 11 June 2011
3. Engelbrech, K.P., Gödde, F., Hartard, F., Ketabdar, H., Möller, S.: Modeling user satisfaction with Hidden Markov Model. In: Matthew, P. (ed.) Proceedings of the SIGDIAL 2009 Conference: The 10th Annual Meeting of the Special Interest Group on Discourse and Dialogue (SIGDIAL 2009), Stroudsburg, PA, USA, pp. 170–177. Association for Computational Linguistics (2009)
4. Sarukkai, R.R.: Real-time user modeling and prediction: examples from Youtube. In: Proceedings of the 22nd International Conference on World Wide Web (WWW 2013 Companion), pp. 775–776. ACM, New York (2013)
5. Salehan, M., Kim, D.J.: Predicting the performance of online consumer reviews: a sentiment mining approach to big data analytics. Decis. Support Syst. **81**, 30–40 (2016). ISSN 0167-9236
6. Proynova, R., Paech, B.: Factors influencing user feedback on predicted satisfaction with software systems. In: Doerr, J., Opdahl, Andreas L. (eds.) REFSQ 2013. LNCS, vol. 7830, pp. 96–111. Springer, Heidelberg (2013). https://doi.org/10.1007/978-3-642-37422-7_7
7. Nourikhah, H., Akbari, M.K.: Impact of service quality on user satisfaction: modeling and estimating distribution of quality of experience using Bayesian data analysis. Electron. Comm. Res. Appl. **17**, 112–122 (2016)
8. Kiseleva, J., Williams, K., Awadallah, A.H., Crook, A.C., Zitouni, I., Anastasakos, T.: Predicting user satisfaction with intelligent assistants. In: Proceedings of the 39th International ACM SIGIR conference (SIGIR 2016), pp. 45–54. ACM, New York (2016)
9. Kim, Y., Hassan, A., Ryen, W., Zitouni, I.: Modeling dwell time to predict click-level satisfaction. In: Proceedings of the 7th ACM International Conference on Web Search and Data Mining (WSDM 2014), pp. 193–202. ACM (2014)
10. Hsieh, W.W., Tang, B.: Applying neural network models to prediction and data analysis in meteorology and oceanography. Bull. Am. Meteorol. Soc. **79**, 1855–1870 (1998)
11. Noh, M.J., Kim, J.S.: Factors influencing the user acceptance of digital home services. Telecommun. Policy **34**(11), 672–682 (2010)
12. Johnson-Laird, P.N.: Deductive reasoning. Annu. Rev. Psychol. **50**(1), 109–135 (1999)
13. Zepernick, H.J., Iqbal, M.I., Khatibi, S.: Quality of experience of digital multimedia broadcasting services: an experimental study. In: IEEE Sixth International Conference on Communications and Electronics (ICCE), Ha Long, pp. 437–442 (2016)
14. Touré, C., Michel, C., Marty, J.-C.: Re-designing knowledge management systems: towards user-centred design methods integrating information architecture. In: Knowledge Management and Information Sharing, Rome, Italy, October 2014

15. Rana, J., Kristiansson, J., Synnes, K.: Enriching and simplifying communication by social prioritization. In: 2010 International Conference on Advances in Social Networks Analysis and Mining, Odense, pp. 336–340 (2010)
16. Brown, T.F., Mowen, J.C., Donavan, D.T., Licata, J.W.: The customer orientation of service workers: personality trait effects on self-and supervisor performance ratings. J. Mark. Res. **39** (1), 110–119 (2002)
17. O'Leary, D.E.: User participation in a corporate prediction market. Decis. Support Syst. **78**, 28–38 (2015)
18. Chen, M.K., Wang, S.-C.: The critical factors of success for information service industry in developing international market: using analytic hierarchy process approach. Expert Syst. Appl. **37**(1), 694–704 (2010)
19. Park, J.-H., Kim, Y.B., Kim, M.-K.: Investigating factors influencing the market success or failure of IT services in Korea. Int. J. Inf. Manag. **37**(1, Part A), 1418–1427 (2017). ISSN 0268-4012
20. Peng, F., Schuurmans, D.: Combining Naive Bayes and *n*-gram language models for text classification. In: Sebastiani, F. (ed.) ECIR 2003. LNCS, vol. 2633, pp. 335–350. Springer, Heidelberg (2003). https://doi.org/10.1007/3-540-36618-0_24
21. James, G., Witten, D., Hastie, T., Tibshirani, R.: An Introduction to Statistical Learning. STS, vol. 103. Springer, New York (2013). https://doi.org/10.1007/978-1-4614-7138-7
22. Le, Q.V., Ng, A.Y., et al.: Building high-level features using large scale unsupervised learning. In: Proceedings of the 29 th International Conference on Machine Learning, Edinburgh, Scotland, UK (2012)
23. Kingma, D.P., Ba, J.L.: ADAM: a method for stochastic optimization. In: ICLR (2015)
24. Applen, J.D.: Tacit knowledge, knowledge management, and active user participation in Web site navigation. IEEE Trans. Prof. Commun. **45**(4), 302–306 (2002)

Effective Management of Information Processes with CMS in Smart City. The Concept of Crowdsourcing

Łukasz Przysucha[✉]

Wroclaw University of Economics and Business,
Komandorska 118/120, 53-345 Wroclaw, Poland
lukasz.przysucha@ue.wroc.pl

Abstract. Globalization and civilization development are progressing in the world, according to statistics people have been migrating from rural areas to cities for many years. At the moment, this phenomenon is noticeable in every place and country, regardless of the state of affluence, level of development or other factors. Some developed countries such as Japan have urbanization at 97.6%. Along with the development of cities, problems also arise. One of the largest is the management of large municipal units. It should be noted that in addition to ordinary areas such as public transport and clean air, there are also extremely important as urban community management. Smart City concepts are created to coordinate activities in urban areas, but also outline development directions for the future. The author focuses on the analysis of information processes in Smart City and proper knowledge management thanks to electronic tools such as Resident Portal. Only fully coordinated and properly managed communication between residents, stakeholders and municipal authorities is able to strengthen and develop cities.

Keywords: Knowledge management · Content management systems · Smart City · Crowdsourcing · Information processes

1 Introduction

The idea of a Smart City is a relatively new concept implemented and used by central and local government authorities, business entities and urban residents themselves [1]. An intelligent city is one that uses information communication technologies (ICT) to increase the interactivity and efficiency of urban infrastructure and its components, as well as to raise the awareness of residents [2]. The area of urban and agglomeration development is currently a strategic element of globalization and civilization in the world. The trend of inhabiting urbanized areas on a global scale is more and more dynamic. In 1950, only 30% of the total population lived in cities, now it is almost 55%, while in 2050 it will be over 65% of the population [3] (note the overall global population increase). More and more mega cities are emerging with a population of over 10 million inhabitants. Currently, the most urbanized regions include North America (83% of residents living in cities in 2016), Latin America and the Caribbean (80%) and Europe (73%). The inhabitants of Africa and Asia live mainly in rural areas,

© IFIP International Federation for Information Processing 2020
Published by Springer Nature Switzerland AG 2020
E. Mercier-Laurent (Ed.): AI4KM 2018, IFIP AICT 588, pp. 65–76, 2020.
https://doi.org/10.1007/978-3-030-52903-1_6

at present 40% and 48% of their population live in urban areas. A continuous increase in urban population is forecast in the next decades. Africa and Asia are urbanizing faster than other regions, and according to forecasts, by 2050 they will reach 56% and 64% of urban population, respectively. It is expected that India, China and Nigeria - together will account for 37% of the projected increase in the global urban population in 2014–2050. The estimated population increase [4] in urban areas in India is 404 million inhabitants, in China 292 million and Nigeria 212 million. Tokyo is currently the largest city in the world with an agglomeration of 38 million inhabitants, followed by Delhi with 25 million inhabitants and Shanghai with 23 million inhabitants. Mexico, Mumbai and São Paulo has over 21 million inhabitants. It is estimated that by 2030, 41 megacities with over 10 million inhabitants will be created in the world. Forecasts indicate that Tokyo it will remain the largest city in the world in 2030, with 37 million inhabitants, followed by Delhi, where the population is expected to grow rapidly to 36 million [5].

The development of urban agglomerations has many positive aspects for our civilization, but it is accompanied by many problems. The main of them focuses on proper city management. The author proposes to support knowledge management and knowledge acquisition by using crowdsourcing in the Smart City area. The diffusion of knowledge between decision-makers, shareholders and residents is extremely important because it can significantly help in the communication of all parties, decision-makers will reduce the information gap, and residents and stakeholders, i.e. in a direct understanding, the crowd will be aware of the Smart City environment and will be able to interact with decision makers.

The article is divided into four parts: the first defines information cycle management on the example of a city area, the second discusses the use of content management systems (CMS) as support for knowledge management processes. Then the author discussed the idea of Smart City. The last chapter focuses on obtaining information using crowdsourcing. The author asks the question where is the place of crowdsourcing in the flow and distribution of knowledge in the area of Smart City.

2   Management of Information Processes in Smart City

An intelligent city is a very complex creation, both in terms of infrastructure, communication and logistics as well as multidimensional in terms of information flow [6]. The information process can be called an economic process that performs at least one of the following functions: generating information, gathering information, storing information, processing information, providing information, sharing information, interpreting information or using information [7]. In relation to smart cities, these are all processes that operate on the information they have. The process may be, for example, information sent by delayed buses in the city to all target recipients, i.e. an electronic municipal information system located at city stops as well as the Internet. This information will be emitted and modified for end users - the application estimating the arrival of the nearest vehicle may modify the choice of a bus for another. So one information entails another, so the information cycle is created. Aggregated information may affect subsequent actions, e.g. a delay message will also be sent to the traffic flow monitoring system in the city, which in turn may propose other communication solutions and tips on unloading traffic jams located on large streets. Only well-integrated tools and channels at all levels of information flow can properly distribute data transfer and support the current and future operation of the entire smart city [8].

The author decided to divide the concept of Smart City into 10 spheres that are integral with each other and are responsible for other areas of everyday life of citizens in the city [9]. These are: smart business, smart human capital, smart management, smart environment, smart transportation, smart IT, smart everyday life & communication, smart care and smart future. Each of these modules contains thousands of information processes that interact with each other, and there are mega-processes between the modules. The following are examples of information processes that can occur in the Smart City concept by modular assignment.

Knowledge in Smart City goes through a cycle that lasts indefinitely. The first stage focuses on acquiring knowledge from the environment. Knowledge is obtained from specific locations and transferred. Decision makers can acquire knowledge from residents, or another exchange of knowledge takes place, e.g. between residents, interveners, etc. The next step is to generate knowledge [10]. Tools supporting knowledge management and learning are useful. A great support also for generating knowledge can be the resident portal operating in a given agglomeration [11], which will support all processes remotely in the electronic aspect [12]. Nowadays, this knowledge is extensive in systems and there is no place for evaluation, only collection and repair [13]. Policy makers must remember about secure access to confidential information [14]. The next step is to evaluate knowledge, sort it, prioritize and eliminate unnecessary content. Dedicated aggregation of staff rates by importance, followed by the dissemination of knowledge. The last two stages are responsible for verifying the correctness of the acquired and processed information and making it available in the event of successful validation results [15]. Below is a diagram illustrating knowledge management cycle processes (Fig. 1).

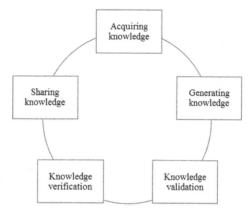

Fig. 1. Knowledge management process. Source: own elaboration.

Information in the Intelligent City is provided in accordance with the standards and procedures set out within a given metropolitan area and imposed IT rules [16]. The content can be divided into text, graphics, charts, videos, animations, and interface of system [17]. Depending on the type of content, there are many ways to aggregate data [18]. Particular attention should be paid to the amount of data stored [19] as it will be necessary to adjust the technical infrastructure and software to data sizes [20]. The scheme of information lifecycle is set out below (Fig. 2).

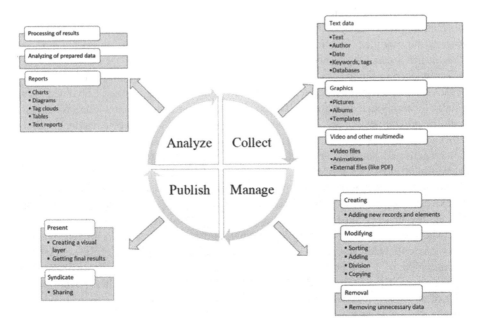

Fig. 2. Content lifecycle. Source: own elaboration.

3   Knowledge Management Systems

Knowledge management is the entire process that enables the creation, dissemination and use of knowledge [21] to achieve the specific goals of an organization [22]. The concept of knowledge management is perceived by modern enterprises, organizations and business entities as one of the elements of building competitive advantage [23]. The methods and strategies of gaining competitive advantage used so far, such as the introduction of new products and continuous improvement of processes, are becoming less and less effective, because products and processes can be easily copied and adapted to the needs of competitive enterprises [24]. Traditional methods require much more effort on the part of employees and costly investments, with a shorter period of using the benefits obtained with their help. Modern realities, i.e. growing competition, rapidly growing customer requirements [25], etc. require the company to provide the highest quality product and an efficient production process.

The author suggests thinking in some respects about the city as a company. A place where economics also works and conditions similar to those in organizations exist. The concept of implementing a knowledge management system in the city can have many positive aspects that will affect the everyday life of residents, as well as in the long term development of urban agglomeration. The following is an analysis of the benefits of implementing knowledge management processes in Smart City from different perspectives suggested by the author.

A. *Business perspective*

The correct flow of information and knowledge, as well as the resulting patterns of appropriate actions can help the creativity of residents, which will result in the creation of new start-up companies, as well as long-term support for local business and the creation of new jobs. Creating unique solutions on a national and global scale can bring companies from other countries to the city, thanks to which patents can also lead to increased profits from city taxes. Additional circumstances conducive to the exchange of knowledge, such as business conferences and meetings of entrepreneurs, can help in the exchange of knowledge between specialists in a given field and residents. The city should allocate funds for such projects.

B. *Educational perspective*

The exchange of knowledge between universities in the city and outside is a key element of their activity. The creation of an information center that collects and disseminates knowledge acquired in metropolises can be a benefit for educational units operating in the Smart City area [26]. Creating models for the exchange of information between scientists, as well as preparing the right conditions for research can be the key to the success of universities and research centers.

C. *Resident perspective*

On the part of the citizen, the exchange of knowledge is important because it allows for self-development, increase of competence and the possibility of raising personal and professional qualifications. This translates into the possibility of better work, and thus potentially increasing the quality of life, as well as supporting urban processes as a partner - residents are able to understand their belonging to the community and engage in urban activities that contribute to the development of the whole society.

D. *Government perspective*

People managing a metropolitan area acquire new qualifications, develop themselves, learn about different perspectives of residents, which allows them to better meet the requirements and support decision-making processes. It is important that the exchange of knowledge take place at all levels in the city and in areas, so that the knowledge resources have interdisciplinary status.

Existing knowledge can be both tacit and explicit. Tacit knowledge [27] exists only in the mind of the person who possesses it, created as a result of experience and not fully aware ("I know I can do it"), manifested only through skillful action. Tacit knowledge is most often transmitted during joint work, workshops, through conversation, storytelling and shared experiences. It is knowledge acquired subconsciously and equally subconsciously used, it is more difficult to express and it is more difficult to write in the form of electronic records. This knowledge can be exchanged in the city by organizing workshops, creating common places to exchange ideas, bringing people together in groups according to professions, industries and hobbies. Explicit knowledge [28] is expressed in character and stored on knowledge carriers. This knowledge can be accumulated in knowledge repositories [29]. For example, cities can have servers connected to a system that has an interface for transferring data and creating workflows, so that data on the other side can be read and properly used in the form of knowledge.

Below, the author provides levels of data, information, knowledge and wisdom, dividing them into tacit and explicit and defining each of them. It is worth noting that the division can be used to create a resident portal, available online, supporting knowledge management processes. On this basis, relevant resources can be assigned and qualified to the persons concerned (Fig. 3).

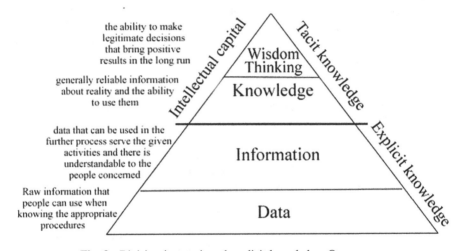

Fig. 3. Division into tacit and explicit knowledge. Own source

Wisdom thinking and knowledge can be defined as intellectual capital. This is an extraordinary positive value [30] for the city. Human and intellectual capital translates directly into the civilization level of the area [31]. People and their understanding of the processes taking place in the world, as well as their skills are the most important instrument in general development.

In December 2018, the author conducted a survey among the inhabitants of the Polish city of Wroclaw. He asked what they associate with the concept of Smart City. The survey was conducted among 200 residents on paper. The gender, age and profession diversity was taken into account (Fig. 4).

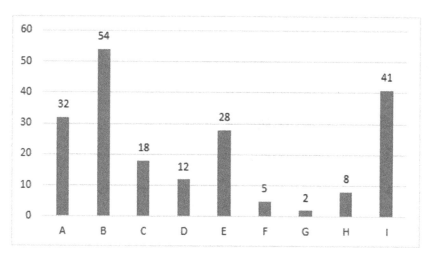

Fig. 4. Associations regarding Smart City. Own source. Chart legend: A - Intelligent public transport. B - New tele information systems, C - Fast Internet. D - Professional health service. E - Clean air and renewable energy sources. F - Social ties. G - Exchange of knowledge. H - Facilitation in shopping. I - Easy contact with the city administration

The survey results show that only 3.5% of respondents associate the idea of Smart City with the creation of a human community and exchange of knowledge between residents. This is a very small result, especially since the Smart City concept aims to change the mentality of residents into action, and not just participation in the passive form. As many as 27% of respondents associate Smart City with modern ICT systems. Respondents pointed to an increase in mobility and easier access to e-mail and e-services, as well as an increase in the number of access points with free Internet access in the city, as well as a fast Internet connection. Over half of the respondents identify Smart City with modern technologies and technical issues related to improving the quality of life. Low awareness of active participation in society as a creator/co-creator of society results in a lack of knowledge sharing processes in society. In turn, the government administration does not receive signals from residents about the need to create knowledge banks, tools supporting the exchange of knowledge and information between residents of a given metropolitan area, which causes the lack of implementation of such solutions.

During this study, the author asked the open question what residents expect in the exchange of knowledge. Answers are shown below (Fig. 5).

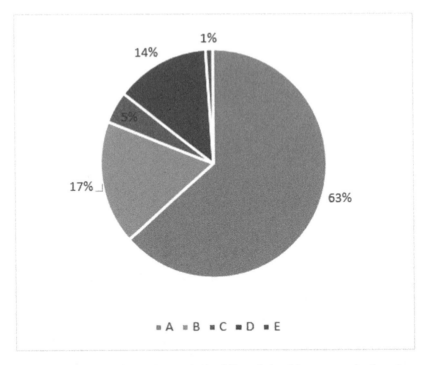

Fig. 5. Expectations of residents in the field of Knowledge Management in the urban area. Chart legend: A - On-line portal for knowledge exchange within the city. B - Events and meetings dedicated thematically for individual groups of residents. C - Stationary places, allowing coming and acquiring general knowledge, interdisciplinary. D - Knowledge base as a material value for the city and its future generations. E - Exchange of knowledge with other unconventional media such as local newspapers and radio

As in the previous study, the sample was 200 people. Most, because 127 respondents replied that they would like to create an Internet portal that will support knowledge among residents. The current trend of transferring all activities to the network and a high degree of mobility are conducive to the development of such initiatives. 63% of respondents would like to contribute to the exchange of knowledge on the network, putting their own neighbourhood and city as a community. Then 17% of residents would like to create events and meetings for thematic groups. Another place was to create a knowledge base that would aggregate data and procedures and benefit future generations. Answers were also received: stationary places for acquiring general knowledge, interdisciplinary and exchange of knowledge with other unconventional media, such as local newspapers and radio. All these activities can lead to the exchange of knowledge in the city, increase public awareness of the smart concept and increase the development of the region.

4 Crowdsourcing as a Tool for Acquiring Knowledge

The subject of crowdsourcing is a fairly new and undiscovered research area. When analyzing literature, there are only a few books on the market that are commercially used for crowdsourcing. There is a research gap in the use of crowdsourcing at the urban community level. The literature on the subject focuses mainly on scientific articles, the intensification of which can be attributed to 2018 and 2019.

Crowdsourcing is a process in which an organization (a company, public institution, non-profit organization) commissions tasks traditionally performed by employees of an unidentified, usually very wide group of people in the form of an open connection [33]. It is worth noting that the latest definitions are beginning to open to other entities and areas, not only those related to organizations and business. The potential of crowdsourcing in public aspects has been recognized, addressing a wider society.

The main advantages of crowdsourcing over the urban community may include [34]:

1. Saves time and money (the crowd generates ideas much faster, and preparing a website is definitely cheaper than paying for a narrow, specialized team) [35].
2. Variety of submitted projects and their originality (many perspectives and points of view).
3. Obtaining information about the needs and expectations of residents.
4. Creating an engaged community.
5. Marketing and promotional benefits.

The most important research questions that focus on learning factors:

1. What factors determine the involvement of stakeholders in acquiring knowledge?
2. What tools are used to acquire knowledge from stakeholders?
3. To what extent and scope can the acquired knowledge be used in Smart City projects?

Below the author presents a general scheme of knowledge distribution in the area of Smart City, including Crowdsourcing of tasks (Fig. 6).

The author has created a diagram illustrating the distribution of knowledge and information in the area of Smart City. Crowdsourcing is the answer to the lack of knowledge. Enforces commitment directly related to motivation. It is extremely important to observe the factors affecting the willingness to share knowledge of residents and to answer the question of what elements contribute to increasing the motivation of participants.

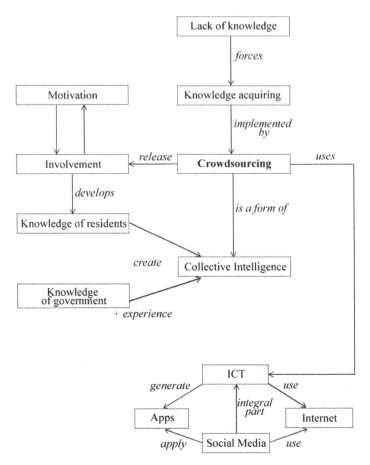

Fig. 6. Semantic network presenting crowdsourcing contexts as methods of acquiring knowledge.

5   Conclusion

The article focuses on the role of the Smart City idea in current time, as well as the use of tools such as Crowdsourcing to optimize information exchange processes and knowledge management in metropolitan areas. The author carried out a study showing that there is a very high demand for electronic services that will support communication between residents, decision makers and stakeholders, as well as services supporting digital management of all areas of the city. The article cites the benefits of implementing knowledge management processes in the Smart City area from various perspectives, including business, education, resident and government. The article cites the benefits of implementing knowledge management processes in the Smart City area from various perspectives, including business, education, resident and government.

Resident portal tools available on-line for all urban groups can connect all Smart City zones, mediate communication that can be used for Crowdsourcing and manage information processes in urban agglomerations.

References

1. Owoc, M., Marciniak, K.: Knowledge management as foundation of smart university. In: 2013 Federated Conference on Computer Science and Information Systems, pp. 1267–1272. IEEE (2013)
2. Abu-Tayeh, G., Neumann, O., Stuermer, M.: Exploring the motives of citizen reporting engagement: self-concern and other-orientation. Bus. Inf. Syst. Eng. **60**, 215–226 (2018)
3. Wang, J., Zhao, J., Zhang, Y., Peng, X., Li, Y., Xie, Y.: Enabling Human-Centric Smart Cities: Crowdsourcing-Based Practice in China. Peking University, China (2018)
4. Papadopoulou, C., Giaoutzi, M.: Crowdsourcing and Living Labs in Support of Smart Cities' Development, Greece (2019)
5. Ghezzi, A., Gabelloni, D., Martini, A., Natalicchio, A.: Crowdsourcing: A Review and Suggestions for Future Research. British Academy of Management/Wiley (2018)
6. Rothe, R., Rutkowska, M., Sulich, A.: Smart cities and challenges for European integration. In: Proceedings of the 4th International Conference on European Integration 2018, ICEI 2018, Ostrava, Czech Republic, vol. 3, pp. 1240–1246 (2018)
7. Weichbroth, P., Brodnicki, K.: The lemniscate knowledge flow model. In: 2017 Federated Conference on Computer Science and Information Systems (FedCSIS), pp. 1217–1220. IEEE (2017)
8. Weichbroth, P.: Mining e-mail message sequences from log data. In: 2018 Federated Conference on Computer Science and Information Systems (FedCSIS), pp. 855–858. IEEE (2018)
9. Przysucha, L.: Knowledge management processes in Smart City-electronic tools supporting the exchange of information and knowledge among city residents. Int. J. Innov. Manag. Technol. **10**(4), 155–160 (2019)
10. Mercier-Laurent, E., Jakubczyc, J., Owoc, M.L.: What is knowledge management? Prace Naukowe Akademii Ekonomicznej we Wrocławiu **815**, 9–21 (1999)
11. Kusio, E.: Kształtowanie programu projektów ITS–studium przypadku. Przedsiębiorstwo we współczesnej gospodarce – teoria i praktyka **21**(2), 115–129 (2017)
12. Wirkus, M., Kusio, E.: Elementy zarządzania operacyjnego ruchem drogowym w miastach. Studia Ekonomiczne Regionu Łódzkiego 361–377 (2017)
13. Kusio, E.: Inteligentne wspomaganie zarządzania operacyjnego ruchem drogowym. Transport Miejski i Regionalny (2017)
14. Wirkus, M., Kusio, E.: Zarządzanie interesariuszami jako czynnik sukcesu innowacyjnego projektu. Manag. Sci. (Nauki O Zarzadzaniu) **28**(3) (2016)
15. Owoc, M.L., Ochmanska, M., Gladysz, T.: On principles of knowledge validation. In: Vermesan, A., Coenen, F. (eds.) Validation and Verification of Knowledge Based Systems, pp. 25–35. Springer, Boston (1999). https://doi.org/10.1007/978-1-4757-6916-6_2
16. Domagała, P.: Internet of Things and Big Data technologies as an opportunity for organizations based on knowledge management. In: Proceedings of ICMIMT 2019, Cape Town, South Africa, pp. 199–203 (2019)
17. Weichbroth, P., Redlarski, K., Garnik, I.: Eye-tracking web usability research. In: 2016 Federated Conference on Computer Science and Information Systems (FedCSIS), pp. 1681–1684. IEEE (2016)

18. Pondel, M., Korczak, J.: A view on the methodology of analysis and exploration of marketing data. In: 2017 Federated Conference on Computer Science and Information Systems (FedCSIS), pp. 1135–1143. IEEE (2017)

19. Pondel, M., Pondel, J.: Big Data solutions in cloud environment. In: FedCSIS Position Papers, pp. 233–238 (2016)

20. Pondel, M., Korczak, J.: Recommendations based on collective intelligence – case of customer segmentation. In: Ziemba, E. (ed.) AITM/ISM -2018. LNBIP, vol. 346, pp. 73–92. Springer, Cham (2019). https://doi.org/10.1007/978-3-030-15154-6_5

21. Kanagasabapathy, K.A., Radhakrishnan, R., Balasubramanian, S.: Empirical investigation of critical success factor and knowledge management structure for successful implementation of knowledge management system – a case study. In: Process Industry, Hindustan College of Engineering Review, pp. 2–3 (2000)

22. Owoc, M., Weichbroth, P.: Validation model for discovered web user navigation patterns. In: Mercier-Laurent, E., Boulanger, D. (eds.) AI4KM 2012. IAICT, vol. 422, pp. 38–52. Springer, Heidelberg (2014). https://doi.org/10.1007/978-3-642-54897-0_3

23. Matouk, K., Owoc, M.L.: A survey of data warehouse architectures—preliminary results. In: 2012 Federated Conference on Computer Science and Information Systems (FedCSIS), pp. 1121–1126. IEEE (2012)

24. Kubiak, B. F., Weichbroth, P.: Cross-and up-selling techniques in e-commerce activities, eCommerce, ePayments and new entrepreneurship 15(3), 1–7 (2010)

25. Ossowska, K., Szewc, L., Weichbroth, P., Garnik, I., Sikorski, M.: Exploring an ontological approach for user requirements elicitation in the design of online virtual agents. In: Wrycza, S. (ed.) SIGSAND/PLAIS 2016. LNBIP, vol. 264, pp. 40–55. Springer, Cham (2016). https://doi.org/10.1007/978-3-319-46642-2_3

26. Girard, J., Girard, J.A.: Defining knowledge management: toward an applied compendium. Online J. Appl. Knowl. Manag. 3(1), 4 (2015)

27. Wyatt, J.C.: Management of explicit and tacit knowledge. J. R. Soc. Med. 94, 6 (2001)

28. Smith, E.A.: The role of tacit and explicit knowledge in the workplace. J. Knowl. Manag. 5, 315 (2001)

29. Weichbroth, P., Owoc, M., Pleszkun, M.: Web user navigation patterns discovery from WWW server log files. In: 2012 Federated Conference on Computer Science and Information Systems (FedCSIS), pp. 1171–1176. IEEE (2012)

30. Mercier-Laurent, E.: Managing intellectual capital in knowledge economy. In: Mercier-Laurent, E., Owoc, M.L., Boulanger, D. (eds.) AI4KM 2014. IAICT, vol. 469, pp. 165–179. Springer, Cham (2015). https://doi.org/10.1007/978-3-319-28868-0_10

31. Hołowińska, K.: Selected knowledge management aspects in modern education. In: Mercier-Laurent, E., Boulanger, D. (eds.) AI4KM 2017. IAICT, vol. 571, pp. 29–39. Springer, Cham (2019). https://doi.org/10.1007/978-3-030-29904-0_3

32. Brabham, D.C.: Crowdsourcing as a model for problem solving an introduction and cases. Converg.: Int. J. Res New Media Technol. 14, 75–90 (2008)

33. Brabham, D.C.: Crowdsourcing. The MIT Press, New York (2013)

34. Ghezzi, A., Gabelloni, D., Martini, A., Natalicchio, A.: Crowdsourcing: a review and suggestions for future research. IJMR 20(2), 343–363 (2018)

35. Zema, T., Sulich, A.: Relations in the interorganizational networks. Int. J. Soc. Sci. Educ. Stud. 6(1), 111–121 (2019)

A Naming System for "The Internet of Things" Adapted to Industry - A Case Study in Electrical Engineering

Anne Dourgnon$^{(\boxtimes)}$ and Tuan Dang

EDF R&D, Chatou, France
{anne.dourgnon, tuan.dang}@edf.fr

Abstract. The development of information systems (IS) in the field of electrical engineering represents a significant challenge: virtual reality has to be explicit and remain true to the functional and behavioral perception of real industrial objects. The digitization of processes, names and functions is, in any case, not all that simple. One needs to study reality to understand the underlying cognitive representations. This paper presents two points that we feel are important: the denomination of computer objects in relation to their real-world correspondence and the functional representation within the IS.

Keywords: Industrial Information System · IIS · Industry 4.0 · IoT · IIoT · Conceptual representation · Functional representation · Semantic issue

1 Introduction

As part of the digital transformation process in the era of what is called "Industry 4.0" we are investigating the cognitive representation of industrial equipment by field operators in a power plant. This investigation will allow us to create a better representation of an equipment, designated as "object" thereafter in the industrial information system so that its conceptual model reflects as better as possible its cognitive representation in the mind of field operators. The naming convention of an industrial equipment in the Industrial Information System (IIS) plays an important role in such representation and it reflects an implicit understanding of how an equipment is integrated and interact with the whole industrial process. From our experience, we observe that in existing practices, the designation of objects is tightly linked to the perception of the object in its environment. This is contrary to the view point of Ashton when he talked about the Internet of Things (IoT): "Ideas and information are important, but things matter much more" (Ashton 2009).

The ideas and information about the object manipulated count much more during the evolution of the IIS because they are durable whereas things are changing depending on their revamping.

With this in mind, we feel that it would be impossible to develop Industrial IoT (IIoT) without taking into account two fundamental points about the cognitive representations:

© IFIP International Federation for Information Processing 2020
Published by Springer Nature Switzerland AG 2020
E. Mercier-Laurent (Ed.): AI4KM 2018, IFIP AICT 588, pp. 77–90, 2020.
https://doi.org/10.1007/978-3-030-52903-1_7

- The first point concerns the designation of objects: relational vs position names.
- The second point concerns functional point of view: devices that cannot be represented 'as is' in the IS.

Naming convention should take into account these two points to help field operators to understand physical, behavioral and functional role of the equipment/device.

In the following chapters we will use examples to address these two points and present the lessons learned while developing intelligent IS dedicated to electrical engineering in power plants. We conclude our paper with the description of challenges which still need to be resolved.

2 "The Internet of Things"

In their paper about "The Internet of Things", Gershenfeld, Krikorian and Cohen (Gershenfeld et al. 2004) consider "Naming is one of the primary functions of servers". They distinguished five names: "A networked computer has five different names: a hardware Media Access Control (MAC) for the physical address on the local network (such as "00:08:74:AC:05:0C"), an IP address on the global network ("18.7.22.83"), a network name ("www.mit.edu"), a functional name ("the third server from the left") and the name of a cryptographic key to communicate with it securely". Naming is indeed a key point in IIoT: an efficient codification of name helps to quickly identify the devices.

Let's take an example of the Instrumentation & Control (I&C) of a hydroelectric power generation unit. In this example, the I&C functionalities are done by Alstom's Controbloc automation cells. Let's see how the codification of names is done.

2.1 Relational Names of Devices

Figure 1 shows the excerpt of I&C's schema concerning the Controbloc controller. A controller has many names.

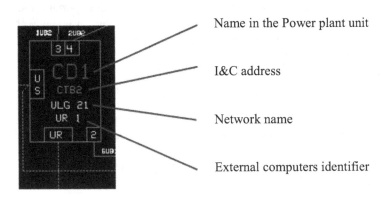

Fig. 1. Names of the controller in a hydraulic power plant's I&C schema.

In this example, we can see that four names are used to designate the same device: CD1, CTB2, ULG21 and UR1.

Let's take the first name. The controller is designated as CD1: Controller "Deux" (Two) of group No. 1. This name is formed from the name "Controbloc" and the name of the Power Plant unit with which it is associated: here, hydraulic unit No. 2. This is a *relational name* –or *associative name*.

What matters here is the relationship between the I&C device and other devices in a given environment and context: the hydraulic groups, the control or display units, the network and the computers. All this four names are expressing relationships with the environment.

For Gershenfeld an al., it's a functional name ("the third server from the left"). We will see in next paragraph (2) what a functional name is for us.

This codification of names is said "*dynamic*" as it reflects the operating mode of I&C system. Generally speaking, it appears that the systems of relational names are dynamic and reflecting *a continuous nature* of functional interaction between devices of a system. These interactions are due to functional links.

If no functional links does exist, no dynamic relation is to be created. This error is sometimes found in models. For example, the relation between a cover and a tub does not exist (Fig. 2).

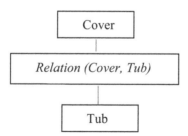

Fig. 2. Example of relation between a cover and a tub.

The relation between Cover and Tub is artificial and, in fact, can evolve. For example, a fitting cover can be introduced. So, definitely, this relation is not an object.

2.2   Position Names of Devices

Let's go in the hydraulic power plant, in the "real world". Figure 3 is a photo showing the top of a Controbloc Controller. You can see that this Controller has two names: it is identified as "CG1", on the left, and by "04 KAS 001 AR", on the right.

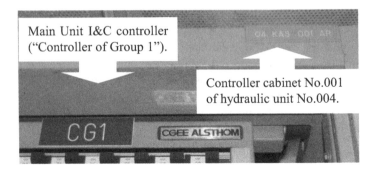

Main Unit I&C controller
("Controller of Group 1").

Controller cabinet No.001
of hydraulic unit No.004.

Fig. 3. Example of position names used for the identification of an I&C cabinet.

These two names have their own specific meaning.

CG1. The designation on the left "CG1" means: Unit main Controbloc. This name specifies that the Controbloc cabinet is *general* (main server), not *local* (slave servers). It's the name used by the hydroelectric power operators.

It is coded and reads from left to right:

– "C" for Controbloc.
– "G" for "Group" and not for "General" (A "General Controbloc" is also referred to as a "Common Controbloc" and is designated as "C").
– "1" for primary, as opposed to secondary, which is designated as "2".

In this hydroelectric power plant, the controllers are not assimilated to I&C nor I&C to the Controbloc automation cells. The designation "CG1" explicitly mentions the Controbloc automation cells.

This name is not a relational name as CD1. Here, in the hydraulic power plant, people see *where* the controller is (near the hydraulic unit No. 4). But they need to know which one of the Controbloc it is: it's the main Controbloc.

04 KAS 001 AR. On the right, "04 KAS 001 AR" is an identification code: it is a technical designation referred to as the equipment system ID number. It is easily read from right to left; it is controller cabinet No. 1 of hydraulic unit[1] No. 4:

– "AR" stands for cabinet (ARmoire, in French).
– "001" is the cabinet number.
– "KAS": The KAS code is derived from the coding "K", for plant "core" and "AS" for controllers. For hydroelectric power plant operators, the KAS code represents "everything connected to the Controbloc".
– "04" represents hydraulic unit No. 04.

These equipment system ID numbers are part of an identification coding system borrowed from the nuclear power field and transposed here in the hydroelectric power field. The essential part of this designation is not its immediate meaning but rather its

---

[1] Hydraulic unit = turbine + generator.

identification capability. In this respect, it is similar to the taxa of the nomenclature applied to living organisms (Simpson 1961). This identification code relates to extrinsic implicits and groups together codes (AR, KAS), which seem as strange to us as do the Latin names of plants. That does not mean they are meaningless. They have meaning in a whole system context.

Relative or Absolute References. In this I&C example, we note two systems of non-redundant names: the relational (or associative) names that correspond to *relative references* (used in the **information** system) as well as position names that correspond to *absolute references* (these are physical markers that actually exist in the field). Relational names are surnames, in the sense of supernumerary: additional name.

Relational names are dynamic, position names are in contrary said "*static*" as they do not reflect any interaction between devices. This fixed positions identification system could be qualified as *a discontinuous system*.

It is interesting to note that depending on the environment in which devices are deployed and thus their designation by users are very different. Concerning the example of Controbloc controller, in a hydroelectric power unit, some Controbloc are said "general" and some are said "local". This difference does not exist in nuclear I&C where Controbloc controllers are also used.

So, when we compare to the five given names of the IoT, we see that the "real world" is much more complex.

2.3   Relational Names and Position Names Are Complementary

Here's another hydroelectric power generation example. The valves are mainly large water control valves as shown here (Fig. 4).

Fig. 4. Head valve of the Lau Balagnas hydroelectric power plant. ©EDF – Gilles de Fayet

Let's see the designation of the valves. The Engineering Team gave us a classification of all the valves (see below, left-hand column). In this classification are listed all the types of valves of the hydraulic power plant. The position names: "Spillway valve", "Head valve"... coexist with the relational names "main system", "auxiliary system". We note that it is not the *type* of valve that matters but its *position* (head...) and its relation with its environment.

A digitization process was launched and, after digitization (right-hand column), most relational names have disappeared, because they have been considered obvious. Now there is no easy way to review the relationship between these valves (Table 1).

Table 1. Classification of valves before and after digitization in the IS.

Classification of Valve before digitization	Classification of Valve after digitization

- main system
   o main valve
      o spillway valve
      o head valve
      o intake valve
   o secondary valve
      o stone trap drain valve
      o water chamber drain valve
      o etc.
- auxiliary system
   o main valve
      o water valve
      o oil valve
      o air valve
   o secondary valve
      o water valve
      o oil valve
      o air valve
- other control systems
   o main valve
      o water valve
      o oil valve
      o air valve
   o secondary valve
      o water valve
      o oil valve
      o air valve
	- spillway valve
	- head valve
	- intake valve
	
	- secondary valve (stone trap drain valve, water chamber drain valve, etc.)
	
	- auxiliary system main water or oil valve
	- auxiliary system main air valve
	
	- other water valve
	- other oil valve
	- other air valve

The position names and the relational names naturally coexist in our cognitive representations. The classification before digitization clearly highlights this duality. The relational names and the position names are complementary and relational names should be conserved, even if they seem obvious. These two aspects must thus be maintained in IIoT, while taking care to make this information explicit. Otherwise, there is a risk that this knowledge may be lost as well as the risk of incompatibility of the designations used by the various IS.

The use of relational and position names are rather well adapted to the devices and equipment: the system is structural. We will see that the designation of things by their functional names is also a key issue in the IS.

3   Functional Names

3.1   Structural vs. Functional Domain

The IoT let us think that everything is "object" and could be designed by relational and/or position names. We think that it's not always the case.

Indeed, the second important point of our feedback concerns structural vs functional systems.

Thermal Units. In the thermal units (fossil-fuel power generation plants), we build from scratch with standard devices plants which will realize energetic functions. The representation is "object oriented" and is moreover the one of the IoT.

These plants relies on a structuring system that conceptualizes the equipment. The standard devices have an identification code: French ECS (EDF Coding System) and German KKS (Kraftwerk Kennzeichensystem) for example. These coding systems strongly differentiate the equipment. The input for the design of the functions is these equipment codes.

On another side, expertise in exploiting hydraulic resources has been developed over thousands of years. Nature "offers" functions: waterfall and stream to which the infrastructures should be adapted. The waterfall or the stream do not have "tags". They are just there.

Hydroelectric Units. In hydroelectric power plants, we adapt to natural and geographic constraints and construct specific plants: mountains, valley and water are each time different! We have functions and we adapt equipment to these functions. Then, the relation between equipment is required first: main system, main valve. And second, the position relative to the function: "Head valve" means in fact "Head valve of the waterfall". An engineer told us that from an hydraulic power plant to another, he had to learn again everything: the relations between systems and the positions of the equipment do change. The waterfall itself does not have a tag, but the position of the equipment does.

Structural or Functional? It is not obvious to know whether or not a domain naturally falls within an object representation or a functional representation.

In the thermal units, equipment are strongly differentiated but functions are not. Equipment may be included in several functions (a kind of overlap). The functions are artificially drawn. One of the goals is to define functional "human-size" systems: when a plant system features more than 9 sub-functions, the system is no longer considered "human sized". The delineation of functions is therefore accompanied by breakdown rules, for example: "The creation of elementary systems having less than 10 actuators or sensors shall be avoided". Contrary to what takes place in hydroelectric power production plants, the delineations of the functions of these systems are not natural as they are simply not easy to grasp.

It is different for hydraulic power plants. In the turbine handbook, the input is a list of all the parameters of the natural functions (rate of flow…). Facing these parameters are the turbine characteristics which are needed. A few turbines are listed, with a lot of technical characteristics.

In the building and operation of hydroelectric power plants, the functional representation of equipment counts much more than the object representation of things because most of the time, things have to be adapted to the environmental and geographical constraints to realize such elementary functions to achieve final expected functions, taking the example of «waterfall» and "stream" to which the infrastructures should be adapted. There is little similarity between two generation plants. In this field, the representation is functional.

Conversely, in the building and operation of thermal power generation plant, the designation of things by their relational and position names is more dominant. Indeed, things are much more standardized in thermal power plants, and similarity is very present.

3.2   Functional Conceptualization

Water Supply and Dam. Let's take a look at the hydroelectric power plants along a valley. It is highly structured into functional assemblies as shown in the following figure «which is a graphical representation of all dams» (Fig. 5).

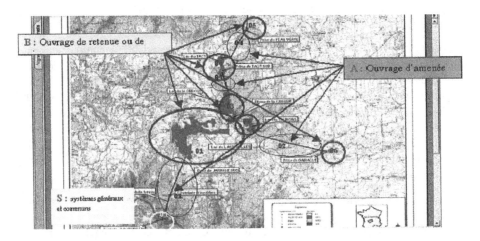

Fig. 5. Description of hydraulic structures.

The functional sets are the following:

- A: everything which supply water,
- B: everything which stop the water,
- S: general systems.

As this diagram shows, the functional sets are strongly differentiated. They are often symbolized by manufactured objects: supply line, retaining structure or dam, etc. (Fig. 6).

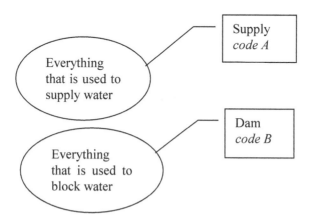

Fig. 6. Two examples of functional groups.

The manner in which the labelling is shown may lend one to think that these sets are equipment. Based on Lévi-Strauss studies, we would point out that it is the privilege of the highly differentiated functional representations to be labelled in this manner. These manufactured objects are themselves the remnants of functional groups maybe owing to the ancient history of hydraulic techniques. And this may be sometimes confusing.

In order to avoid any misunderstanding, the experts emphasize that these sets are in fact functions. They note: "Supply function", "Dam function", etc. which initially seems a bit odd but correctly reflects the underlying functional conceptualization.

Functional Group. A Functional Group "produces goods and services that others [i.e., other Functional Groups] can only obtain through it." (Lévi-Strauss 1966). These groups thus exchange goods (in other words, equipment) but also services (in other words, transformations).

Let's see the diagram on a smaller scale (Fig. 7).

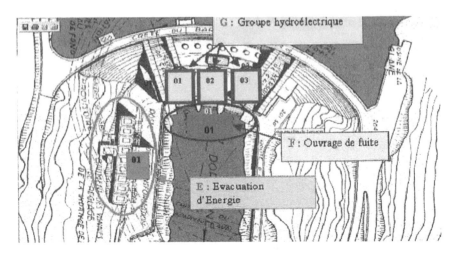

Fig. 7. Description of a dam.

The diagram clearly outlines three functional groups:

– Code G: everything used to produce electricity, symbolized by the hydroelectric units,
– Code F: everything used to return the water to the river, symbolized by the tailrace,
– Code E: everything for power transmission, difficult to symbolize.

We could think that the delimitation of the groups is due to geographical constraints. A technician said: "I know that the breaker of hydroelectric unit No. 1 is there". But which function does the breaker belongs to? hydroelectric unit No. 1? Or the power transmission system?

Greater detail must thus be provided to clearly differentiate the functional assemblies. Also in the following diagram, the expert clearly outlines the functional groups (Fig. 8):

In these highly differentiated systems, "you know where you are, in fact": "you're physically at the dam" because the context is implicitly represented.

Surprises are sometimes encountered in IS when a functional representation is modelled directly on an equipment representation: "someone placed a telecom function on a supply structure since a head valve was equipped with a telephone". In this case, the "telecom" function needs to be differentiated from the "general and common services" function to which it had been assigned.

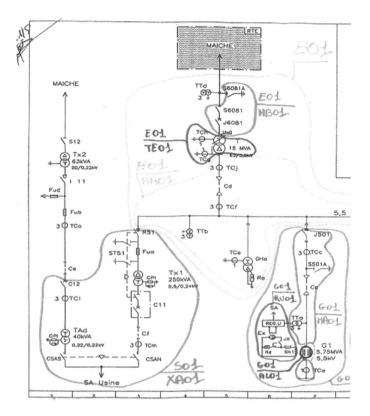

Fig. 8. Functional representation laid out by an expert

Wheel Repair Workshop. Let's consider an example where we are physically in a workshop: here a wheel repair workshop. The planning of this workshop enumerates everything used to repair the wheel of the hydraulic power plant. The planning first describes the wheel around which the functional repair workshop is organized (Table 2).

The system is based on a functional representation where the functions are therefore explicitly formulated. Conversely, the object representations given in the introduction then becomes implicit: wheel, workshop, etc.

Table 2. Wheel repair workshop planning.

Functions	A hydroelectric power plant at the base of a large lake, features 4 vertical-axis Francis turbine generators rated at 90 MW each. It operates at peak performance The turbine wheels weigh 40 tons each and measure 4 m in diameter; they are made of ordinary, non-alloy steel
Planning	The wheels undergo periodic monitoring within the scope of the method
Inspections	Annual inspection with checks of the cavity zones, dye penetrant testing of sensitive points to detect possible cracks and to measure labyrinth clearances
Archiving of inspections	These inspections are recorded on standardized sheets
Weekly analysis of findings	During the last inspection and based on the checks recorded previously, the plant manager noted a change in the size of the cavitation ranges on the wheel of Unit No. 1, along the trailing edges of the vanes, camber side, near the connection with the belt. In addition, the clearances at the lower labyrinths are worse
Weekly selection of interventions	He feels that an intervention on this wheel would be necessary as early as the following year

4 Challenges for IOT

"There are, in fact, only two true models of concrete diversity: one in terms of nature, namely that of the diversity of species; and the other in terms of culture provided by the diversity of functions[2]" (Lévi-Strauss 1966).

Conceptualization is not the same for functional systems and structural models. In order to know which way to use, one must study and understand how it all works.

"There are several reasons why it is complicated for individuals to explain how they work", explains Sophie Le Bellu, who is committed to explaining expert gestures within the scope of her thesis, "work often requires an understanding of the body, incorporated knowledge. Man also has to deal with an undeniable language deficit: there are no words to explain and express everything. Often people start by explaining, then they stop saying "it's complicated". Another phenomenon, the concept of social representations, does not make speaking easy either: the company has an idea of what a given trade involves and the parties concerned themselves are an integral part of this social vision" (Le Bellu 2011).

The inability to express oneself may be associated with not only being unable to find the right words or with taboos (everything relating to one's body in the corporate environment), but also to mental representations that are too obvious to be made aware of: and, as such, they cannot be formulated.

---

[2] Our traduction.

The last reason mentioned, that of the company's social view, should also be included. If the IS takes an opposing view of a trade, by studying it under an object-oriented prism when it is based on functional representation, it becomes difficult for the interested parties to clearly express and formalize their thoughts within the proposed framework. The explanations, the formalizations may be deficient -the expert was unable to adopt the new framework- but they can also become excessive, overflowing the imposed framework: the expert requires notes, diagrams and other additional explanatory tools. Unconsciously, he attempts to re-establish himself within a transformed model.

Then, the explanations that he provides do not stand on their own; they themselves need to be explained. We thus shift from a nearly-wordless model to one that is over-explained. The model of underlying understanding has itself shifted.

Today, we are in the era of the IoT. Following the interconnection of individuals, there is every reason to believe that the objects themselves will be extensively interconnected. But redundancies due to functional mismatch can occur. The progress toward the "digital factory" and the paradigm of the IIoT highlights the object model. However functional representations cannot be converted 'as is'.

The functional representations are somewhat delicate as they feature a very strong conceptual structure, derived from highly-structured technico-economic, and/or organizational, requirements. In the digital factory era, when expertise will no longer be transferred by men, the digital machines must be able to keep track of and justify this conceptualization. This notably wills that the outlines of the functional groups be traced and retained. The functional outline diagrams that trace the history of each installation must be retained.

The virtual world has transformed our way of looking at our real world. The terminology of industrial reality is based on a system of position names while IS essentially use a system of relational names, which interconnects the objects. The two naming systems must nevertheless coexist; one cannot be substituted for the other. And the second point, and possibly the most delicate: certain industrial realities underlie functional conceptualizations that we cannot transpose into a world of objects without distortion.

Communication protocols is an example of massive use of IoT concepts. An interworking framework now includes a semantic level (mostly developed with ontologies) where the naming conventions is a real challenge. That is the difficult question that we have been working on.

The cognitive representation of industrial equipment by field operators in a power plant has to be included in "Industry 4.0". This cognitive representation allows the operators to interact in confidence with digital systems: industrial maintenance can be done "as usual". This requirement should be part of the standards promoted by "Industry 4.0" to guarantee the durability of the systems during the whole life cycle.

References

Ashton, K.: That 'Internet of Things' thing. RFID J. **22**(7), 97–114 (2009)

Chaussecourte, P., Glimm, B., Horrocks, I., Motik, B., Pierre, L.: The energy management adviser at EDF. In: Alani, H., et al. (eds.) ISWC 2013. LNCS, vol. 8219, pp. 49–64. Springer, Heidelberg (2013). https://doi.org/10.1007/978-3-642-41338-4_4

Gershenfeld, N., Krikorian, R., Cohen, D.: The Internet of Things. Sci. Am. **291**, 76–81 (2004)

Lambert, D., Saulwick, A., Nowak, C., Oxenham, M., O'Dea, D.: An Overview of Conceptual Frameworks, Australian Government/Department of Defence, Defence Science and Technology Organisation/Command, Control, Communications and Intelligence Division, Australia (2008)

Lévi-Strauss, C.: The Savage Mind. University of Chicago Press, Chicago (1966)

Le Bellu, S.: Capitalisation des savoir-faire et des gestes professionnels dans le milieu industriel, Mise en place d'une aide numérique au compagnonnage métier dans le secteur de l'énergie. Doctoral thesis, University of Bordeaux II, Bordeaux (2011)

De Saussure, F.: Cours de linguistique générale. Payot, Paris, Nouvelle édition (2005)

Simpson, G.G.: Principles of Animal Taxonomy. Columbia University Press, New York (1961)

Sowa, J.: Knowledge Representation: Logical, Philosophical, and Computational Foundations. Brooks/Cole Publishing Co., Pacific Grove (2000)

Vanlehn, K., Van de Sande, B.: Acquiring conceptual expertise from modeling: the case of elementary physics. In: Anders Ericsson, K. (ed.) Development of Professional Expertise. Toward Measurement of Expert Performance and Design of Optimal Learning Environments, pp. 356–378. Cambridge University Press, New York (2009)

Augmented Learning and Data Filtering: Knowledge Management and Discovery

Cyrus F. Nourani[1]([⊠]) and Eunika Mercier-Laurent[2]

[1] ARDFMTS & Acdmkrd TU Berlin DAI, Berlin, Germany
Acdmkrd@gmail.com
[2] University of Reims Champagne Ardenne, Reims, France
eunika.mercier-laurent@univ-reims.fr

Abstract. Ever since the authors' publications on frontiers of decision trees, forecasting, and business ecosystems, over a decade the techniques for enterprise business systems planning and design with predictive models have become an attention focus. Heuristics on predictive analytics are developed with novel applications to decision trees. Augmented world and priority-based decision trees are new applications for machine learning and big data filtering. The areas addressed include designing predictive modeling with strategic decision systems with applications to analytics, enterprise modeling, and cognitive social media business interfaces. The areas further explored range from plan goal decision tree satisfiability with competitive business models to predictive analytics models that accomplish goals on 3-tier glimpse to business systems. Example decision support application for AI KM with applications is presented. Augmented learning decisions is how AI enhances the decision-making process with more comprehensive cognitive views to business models and infrastructures.

Keywords: Augmented model learning · Data analytics · Decision trees · Predictive analytics · Enterprise modeling · Cognitive spanning

1 Introduction

The areas presented in this paper range from plan goal decision tree satisfiability with competitive business models to predictive analytics models that accomplish goals on a 3-tier business systems design models. The decision-making process for business analytics are explored with an augmentation of decision processes to accomplish goals modeled. Attention spanning trees are applied to focus on plan goal models that can be processed on a vector state machine coupled with a database pre-processor data mining interfaces [33, 38]). Modeling, objectives, and planning issues are examined to present precise decision strategies. Competitive decision tree models are applied to agent learning. Enterprise systems stage sequence communications with business objects and basic content management. Multi-tier interfaces are being explored, focusing on attention spanning [4, 23] with specific examples developed in (Lauth-Nourani-Pederson-Bloom 2013; Lauth 2013). The field of automated learning and discovery has obvious financial and organizational memory applications. There are basic applications to data discovery and model discovery. Augmentation is a process that enhances

© IFIP International Federation for Information Processing 2020
Published by Springer Nature Switzerland AG 2020
E. Mercier-Laurent (Ed.): AI4KM 2018, IFIP AICT 588, pp. 91–106, 2020.
https://doi.org/10.1007/978-3-030-52903-1_8

decision making by providing cognitive decision support that provides AI argumentation that affects behavior and sentiments to make sensible decisions. Hence it does not replace the human decision-making process with an automated machine.

A competitive business modeling technique, based on the first author's planning techniques are stated in brief. Systemic decisions are based on common organizational goals, and as such business planning and resource assignments should strive to satisfy such goals. Heuristics on predictive analytics are examined with brief applications to decision trees. The basic multi-tiered designs are based on the following layers. The presentation layer contains components dealing with user interfaces and user interaction. Example a visual JAVA standalone application. A business logic layer contains components that work together to solve business problems. The data layer is caused by the business logic layer to persist state permanently. More and more enterprises recognize that in the electronically archived databases a there is a potential for knowledge that could be processed up to now only insufficiently example application for competitive models appears in the transactional business models. Alternate models can be designed based on where assets, resources, and responsibility are assigned; how to control and coordination are distributed; and where the plan goals are set. A transactional international business model might comprise a coordinated federation with many assets and resources. The overseas operations are considered a subsidiary to a domestic central corporation. However, decisions and responsibilities are decentralized. Administrative formal management planning and control systems are how headquarters-subdivision controls are managed. Section outlines are as follows: Sect. 2 presents the basics of competitive goals and models. Agent and/or trees are applied as primitives on decision trees to be satisfied by competitive models. Planning with predictive models and goals are presented with stock forecasting examples from the first author's newer decade's publications. The section concludes with the entrepreneurial cognitive augmented decision processes implications. Section 3 briefs on goals, plans, and realizations with data based and knowledge bases. There a function key interface to the database is presented with applications to model discovery and data mining. Competitive model goal satisfiability with model diagrams is briefed with examples. Section 4 presents the applications to decision trees and practical systems design with splitting agent decisions trees. Cognitive spanning with decision trees and state vector machine computations applications are presented. Section 5 presents spanning applications with multitier business interfaces. Social media applications with Gatesense example from the accompanying author's is briefed. The paper concludes with heuristics for competitive models and goals for decision tree accomplishment from the first author's newer game decision tree bases since [12].

2 Competitive Models and Goals

The massive data without data filtering techniques is very prohibitive for business analytics. The process is not based on statistical models for massive data. It is AI that can filter based on data patterns. There is domain knowledge built up from years of experience or technology experts who may be well-versed in data, analytics, or AI. An important AI technique is planning that is based on goal satisfaction at business models. Multiagent planning, for example, as (Muller and Pischel 1994; Bazier et al. [13]), in the paper is modeled as a competitive learning problem where the agents compete on game trees as candidates to satisfy goals hence realizing specific models where the plan goals are satisfied. When a specific agent group "wins" to satisfy a goal the group has presented a model to the specific goal, presumably consistent with an intended world model. For example, if there is a goal to put a spacecraft at a specific planet's orbit, there might be competing agents with alternate micro-plans to accomplish the goal. While the galaxy model is the same, the specific virtual worlds where a plan is carried out to accomplish a real goal at the galaxy via agents are not. Therefore, Plan goal selections and objectives are facilitated with competitive agent learning. The intelligent languages [6, 32] are ways to encode plans with agents and compare models on goal satisfaction to examine and predict via model diagrams why one plan is better than another, or how it could fail. Games play an important role as a basis for economic theories. Here the import is brought forth onto decision tree planning. An agent AND/OR tree is an AND/OR tree e.g. [6], with AND/OR trees from (Nielsen 1967, Genesereth-Nilsson [22]) where the tree branches are intelligent trees. The branches compute a Boolean function via agents. The Boolean function is what might satisfy a goal formula on the tree. An intelligent AND/OR tree is solved iff the corresponding Boolean functions solve the AND/OR trees named by intelligent functions on the trees. Thus node m might be f(a1, a2, a3) & g(b1, b2), where f and g are Boolean functions of three and two variables, respectively, and ai's and bi are Boolean valued agents satisfying goal formulas for f and g.

2.1   Predictive Models

Predictive modeling is an artificial intelligence technique defined since the first author's model-theoretic planning project over a decade before. It is a cumulative nonmonotonic approximation attained with completing model diagrams on what might be true in a model or knowledge base. A predictive diagram for a theory T is a diagram D(M), where M is a model for T, and for any formula q in M, either the function f: q $\rightarrow$ {0,1} is defined, or there exists a formula p in D(M), such that T $\cup$ {p} proves q; or that T proves q by minimal prediction. Prediction involves constructing hypotheses, where each hypothesis is a set of atomic literals; such that when some particular theory T is augmented with the hypothesis, it entails the set of goal literals G. The hypotheses must be a subset of a set of ground atomic predictable. The logical theory augmented with the hypothesis must be proved consistent with the model diagram. Prediction is minimal when the hypothesis sets are the minimal such sets. Plan goal selections and objectives are facilitated with competitive agent learning. The intelligent languages [6, 32] are ways to encode plans with agents and compare models on goal satisfaction to examine and predict via model diagrams why one plan is better than another, or how it could fail. Games play an important role as a basis for economic theories. Here the import is brought forth onto decision tree planning. Newer tree computing techniques are applied to present precise strategies and prove theorems on multiplayer games. Game tree degree concerning models is defined and applied to prove soundness and completeness.

2.2   How Augmented Model Decisions are Permeated

Augmented intelligence combines person and machine intelligence when filtering data for value creation. Augmenting instincts and intuition with AI algorithms render rapid data-driven predictive insights. These insights can help people redesign functions, detect patterns find strategic opportunities, and turn data into action. We have seen some specifics on the preceding sections intended to extend human cognitive abilities, augmented intelligence is different from straight automation.

Augmented world cognitive decision-making involves a creative mix of data, analytics, and artificial intelligence (AI), with a clever person-machine ambient inter-action. The consequent is augmented intelligence with the analytical power and speed of AI managing the big data towards agile, smarter decisions and discovering patterns. The analytics that is deployed at major companies are not yet at the stage that one can state examples for augmented, that is an abstraction, for example to business processes to which one can apply machine intelligence to address lower lever decisions in infrastructure, for example, fall short of their potential. We present some techniques, for example, cognitive spanning for decision making.

2.3   Entrepreneurship Behavior and Decisions Example

Entrepreneurship research [11] focuses on what type of personality entrepreneurs have. Since the activities are new in certain respects the uncertainty and unpredictability are central characteristics of entrepreneurship. Research has shown that certain personality traits correlate to the propensity to engage in entrepreneurship. Gartner (1989) presents bases that behavior, rather than personality traits, that permeate entrepreneurial decision making: to engage or not to engage decisions in certain entrepreneurial activities. When AI and behavior are the considerations the paradigm shift in how man and machine will work together is behavior-driven, therefore, amenable to argumentation. Equally important, you need to have the right models and processes in place, i.e. the recipes for success.

One would like to have APS that processes data with AI and create predictive models to make predictive recommendations e.g. (Nourani 2017 - TUB EM). But these models do not exist in a vacuum. They involve inputs and outputs that impact the rest of your business. You have to think about how these models fit in and how to prioritize the insights from data. Moreover, you need governance over augmented intelligence to see that the automation is working and people know their role in the new man-meets-machine workforce. The innovation ecosystem is based on decision processes that are augmentation critical. Self-regulated innovations inn self-managing teams are additionally important areas for the behavior and decision examples [7] and (Mercier-Laurent 2017) are example overviews for the ecosystem processes on innovations [20] and (Nourani-Lauth-Pedersen 2006) are the past glimpses to the economies for decision processes considered here.

3 Goals, Plans, and Knowledge Bases

Practical systems are designed by modeling with information, rules, goals, strategies, and information onto the data and knowledge bases, where masses of data and their relationships and representations are stored respectively. Example analytics systems on the agenda are Watson Analytics: a cognitive system that sifts through massive data to discover insights that can help its users answers to the most complex of questions. It can reach for relevant answers in the context of questions. Furthermore can become smarter, learning from each interaction with users, and each piece of data it interacted with. Watson can "think" or "reason" similar to a real person. It processes information, draws conclusions, and learns from its experiences.

With our agent augmented decision trees with forward chaining, that is a goal satisfaction technique where inference rules are activated by data patterns, to sequentially get to a goal by applying the inference rules, allows decisions on the surface meta-data on an augmented abstraction with keyed data functions. The current pertinent rules are available at an 'agenda' store. The rules carried out will modify the database. Backward chaining is an alternative based on an opportunistic response to changing information. It starts with the goal and looks for available premises that might be satisfied to have gotten there. Goals are objects for which there is automatic goal generation of missing data at the goal by recursion backward chaining on the missing objects as sub-goals. Data unavailability implies a search for new goal discovery.

A basis to model discovery and prediction planning is presented in [23] and is briefed here. The new AI agent computing business bases defined during the last several years can be applied to present precise decision strategies on multiplayer games with only perfect information between agent pairs. The game trees are applied to improve models. The computing model is based on novel competitive learning with agent multiplayer game tree planning. Specific agents are assigned to transform the models to reach goal plans where goals are satisfied based on competitive game tree learning. The planning applications include OR - ERP and EM as goal satisfiability. Minimal prediction is an artificial intelligence technique defined since the author's model-theoretic planning project. It is a cumulative nonmonotonic approximation attained with completing model diagrams on what might be true in a model or knowledge base.

3.1 Decision-Theoretic Planning

A novel basis to decision-theoretic planning with competitive models was presented in [10, 38, 40] and [27] with classical and non-classical planning techniques, see for example, (Hedeler et al. 1990; Wilkins 1984) from artificial intelligence with games and decision trees providing an agent expressive planning model. We use a broad definition of decision-theoretic planning that includes planning techniques that deal with all types of uncertainty and plan evaluation. Planning with predictive model diagrams represented with keyed KR to knowledge bases is presented. Techniques for representing uncertainty, plan generation, plan evaluation, plan improvement, and are accommodated with agents, predictive diagrams, and competitive model learning.

Modeling with effector and sensor uncertainty, incomplete knowledge of the current state, and how the world operates is treated with agents and competitive models.

Bounds on game trees were developed based on the first author's preceding publications on game trees generalizations on VMK to on [27]. Partial deductions in this approach correspond to proof trees that have free Skolemized trees in their representation. Our past decade developments have applied diagrams do for knowledge discovery knowledge management. Diagrams allow us to model-theoretically characterize incomplete KR. To key into the incomplete knowledge base.

The following figure depicts selector functions Fi from an abstract view grid interfaced via an inference engine to a knowledge base and in turn onto a database.

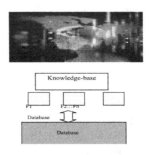

Fig. 1. Keyed data functions, inference, and model discovery. Adapted from [8] & Cognitive MIT Sloan Reviews

Generalized predictive diagrams are defined, whereby specified diagram functions and the search engine can select onto localized data fields. A Generalized Predictive Diagram, is a predictive diagram where D(M) is defined from a minimal set of functions. The predictive diagram could be minimally represented by a set of functions {f1, ..., fn} that inductively define the model. The functions are keyed onto the inference and knowledge base to select via the areas keyed to, designated as Si's in Fig. 1, and data is retrieved Nourani [20]. Visual object views to active databases might be designed with the above. The trees defined by the notion of provability implied by the definition might consist of some extra Skolem functions {g1, ..., gn}, that appear at free trees. The f terms and g terms, tree congruences, and predictive diagrams then characterize deduction with virtual trees Nourani [12] as intelligent predictive interfaces. Data discovery from knowledge diagrams might be viewed as satisfying a goal by getting at relevant data which instantiates a goal. The goal formula states what relevant data is sought.

3.2 Competitive Models and Goal Satisfiability

Business intelligence interfaces might apply automated learning and discovery-often called data mining, machine learning, or advanced data analysis has new w-interface relevance. There are obvious financial and organizational memory applications. E-business, trustworthiness, usability, Human-Computer Interaction, cognitive ergonomics, user interface design, ease of use, interaction design, and online marketing, are the business user modeling issues areas to address. Consider an example ERP system to optimize a business plan with task assignments based on team-play compatibility. Generic model diagrams are basic function-based data modeling techniques the first author put forth over a decade ago to characterize a business domain, with for example [34], business objects on a minimal function base.

Remark: The functions above are those by which a business model could be characterized by some schemes, e.g. stock forecasting scheme example e.g. [35]. The computing specifics are based on creating models from generic model diagram functions where basic models can be piece-meal designed and diagrams completed starting from incomplete descriptions at times. Models uphold to a deductive closure of the axioms modeled and some rules of inference, depending on the theory. By the definition of a diagram, they are a set of atomic and negated atomic sentences. Thus the diagram might be considered as a basis for a model, provided we can by algebraic extension, define the truth value of arbitrary formulas instantiated with arbitrary terms.

4   Decision Trees and Vector Spanning Cognitive Spaces

Game theory is the study of rational behavior in situations in which choices have a mutual effect on one's business and competitors. The best decision depends on what others do, and what others do may depend on what they think you do. Hence games and decisions are intertwined. A second stage business plan needs to specify how to assign resources concerning the decisions, ERP plans, and apply that to elect supply chain policies, which can in part specify how the business is to operate. The splitting agent decision trees have been developed independently by (Nourani ECAI [32]). The computing model is based on novel competitive learning with agent multiplayer game tree planning. For example, when arranging team playing, there are many permutations on where the players are positioned. Every specific player arrangement is a competitive model. There is a specific arrangement that does best in a specific game. What model is best can be determined with agent player competitive model learning.

4.1   Cognitive Learning-Based Decisions

Cognitive agents are software agents included in the higher-level performance of autonomous intelligent systems. They belong to the class of autonomous agents which are complex computing entities active in some kind of environment without the direct intervention of humans or other virtual systems. For an overview on what was our beginning, examples are (Nourani [10, 38, 40]; Nourani et al. 2017). To design intelligent agents systems, flexible problem-solving behavior, and adequate knowledge about the beliefs regarding the environment and its changing conditions is required. We refer here to humans, as well as to virtual systems and we try to look at some general characteristics of new cyber-physical systems. Multi-agent planning is modeled as a competitive learning problem where the agents compete on game trees as candidates to satisfy goals hence realizing specific models where the plan goals are satisfied. Example agenda can distinguish and prioritize Commitments: Committed plans Committed goals Intended goals and Intended plans [25].

4.2 Approaches to Cognitive Systems

Three broad approaches have been adopted so far for implementing cognitive concepts into autonomously acting systems: Data modeling approach that infers the cognitive concepts from the modular data structures to means-end reasoning system through a theorem prover. An example is a cognitive agent system called Artimis [18], an intentional system designed for human interaction and applied in a spoken-dialog interface for human information access. Procedural approaches that use explicit representations of cognitive contents approach based on the BID: belief, intention, desire agent models and can be instantiated in a procedural reasoning system (PRS), like e.g. MARS [18]. Most cognitive systems fall into this second category. The newest approach is the "situated automata" approach that has no explicit representations of the cognitive concepts and therefore seems to perform better than other approaches in settings where higher performance is expected. Cognitive agents are present in complex applications trying to solve efficiently: context-sensitive behavior, adaptive reasoning, ability to monitor and respond to a situation in real-time (immersive agents), and modeling capabilities based on an understanding of human cognitive behavior, like innovation management, generation of new insights, e.g. new ways of thinking. Further application areas are ubiquitous computing so far as person-machine exchanges might be perceived [26]. Example research on cognitive agents are on the first author's publications at CBS Copenhagen, e.g. [10, 38, 40] on affective haptic logic, and (Huhn and Sihng 1988).

4.3 Splitting Trees and the CART Model

The following examples from (Nourani 2010) can be motivating for business applications. Example: A business manager has 6 multitalented players, designed with personality codes indicated with codes on the following balls. The plan is to accomplish 5 tasks with persons with matching personality codes to the task, constituting a team. Team competitive models can be generated by comparing teams on specific assignments based on the task area strength. The optimality principles outlined on the first author's publications might be to accomplish the goal with as few a team grouping as possible, thereby minimizing costs. The following section presents new agent game trees the author had put forth [26]. Applying game theory to business is tantamount to interactive decision theory. Decisions are based on the world as given. However, the best decision depends on what others do, and what others do may depend on what they think you do. Hence games and decisions are intertwined. A second stage business plan needs to specify how to assign resources concerning the decisions, ERP plans, and apply that to elect supply chain policies, which can in part specify how the business is to operate. A tactical planning model that plans critical resources up to sales and delivery is a business planner's dream. Planning and tasking require a definition of their respective policies and processes; and the analyses of supply chain parameters. The above are the key elements of a game, anticipating behavior, and acquiring an advantage. The players on the business planned must know their options, the incentives, and how do the competitors think.

Example premises: Strategic Interactions Strategies: {Advertise, Do Not Advertise} Payoffs: Companies' Profits Advertising costs Euro million. The And vs. Or principle is carried out on the above trees with the System to design ERP systems and manage as Cause principle decisions. The agent business modeling techniques the author had introduced [25, 28] apply the exact 'system as cause' and 'system as symptom' based on models (assumptions, values, etc.) and the 'system vs. symptom' principle via tracking systems behavior with cooperating computational agent trees. The design might apply agents splitting trees, where splitting trees is a well-known decision tree technique. Surrogate agents are applied to splitting trees. The technique is based on the first author's intelligent tree project ECAI 1994 and European AI Communication journal are based on agent splitting tree decisions like what is designed later on the CART system: The ordinary splitting tree decisions are regression-based, developed at Berkeley and Stanford [1], (Breiman 1996).

CART system deploys a binary recursive partitioning that for our system is applications for the agent and/or trees [9, 37]. The term "binary" implies that each group is represented by a "node" in a decision tree, can only be split into two groups. Thus, each node can be split into two child nodes, in which case the original node is called a parent node. The term "recursive" refers to the fact that the binary partitioning process can be applied over and over again. Thus, each parent node can give rise to two child nodes and, in turn, each of these child nodes may themselves be split, forming additional children. The term "partitioning" refers to the fact that the dataset is split into sections or partitioned. CART trees are much simpler to interpret than the multivariate logistic regression model, making it more likely to be practical in a clinical setting. Secondly, the inherent "logic" in the tree is easily apparent.

The agent splitting decision trees have been developed independently since (Nourani [32] - ECAI). For new directions in forecasting and business planning [42]. Team coding example diagram from reach plan optimal games where a project is managed with a competitive optimality principle is to achieve the goals minimizing costs with the specific player code rule first author and company 2005. More recent areas are optimized decisions based on goal reachability [21].

4.4   Designing an Augmented Learning Model Decision Support Systems

The formal compositional framework for modeling multi-agent tasks DESIRE is introduced here. The following aspects are modeled and specified: (1) a task (de)-composition, (2) information exchange, (3) sequencing of (sub)tasks, (4) subtask delegation, (5) knowledge structures. Information required/produced by a (sub)task is defined by input and output signatures of a component. The signatures used to name the information are defined in predicate logic with a hierarchically ordered sort structure (order-sorted predicate logic). Units of information are represented by the ground atoms defined in the signature. The role information plays within reasoning is indicated by the level of an atom within a signature: different (meta) levels may be distinguished.

In a two-level situation, the lowest level is termed object-level information, and the second level meta-level information. Some specifics and a mathematical basis to such models with agent signatures might be obtained from [34]. Meta-level information contains information about object-level information and reasoning processes; for example, for which atoms the values are still unknown (epistemic information). Similarly, tasks that include reasoning about other tasks are modeled as meta-level tasks with respect to object-level tasks. Often more than two levels of information and reasoning occur, resulting in meta-meta-information and reasoning. Information exchange between tasks is specified as information links between components. Each information link relates to output of one component to the input of another, by specifying which truth-value of a specific output atom is linked with which truth value of a specific inputs.

5 Spanning and the Multitier Models

5.1 Spanning Attention on Decision Trees

When a specific agent group "wins" to satisfy a goal, the agent group is presenting a model consistent with an intended world model for that goal. For example, if there is a goal to put a spacecraft at a specific planet's orbit, there might be competing agents with alternate micro-plans to accomplish the goal [38]. While the galaxy model is the same, the specific virtual worlds where a plan is carried out to accomplish a real goal at the galaxy via agents are not. Therefore, plan goal selections and objectives are based on the attention spans with competitive agent learning. This technique can be also used to solve highly interacting communication problems in a complex web application, web intelligence settings. The intelligent languages [3, 32] are ways to encode plans with agents and compare models on goal satisfaction to examine and predict via model diagrams why one plan is better than another, or how it could fail. The state space agent modeling present techniques to span the attention state space, where specific agents with internal state set I can distinguish their membership. State vector machines-SVM, agent vectors, and data mining referring to the sections above are applied to design cognitive spanning. SVM creates a set of hyper-planes in N-dimensional space that is used for classification, regression, and spanning in our approach. The SVM algorithms create the largest minimum distance to have competitive goals satisfied on models.

The BID-architectures upon which specifications for compositional multi-agent systems are based are the result of analysis of the tasks performed by individual agents and groups of agents. Task (de)compositions include specifications of interaction between subtasks at each level within a task (de)composition, making it possible to explicitly model tasks that entail interaction between agents. The formal compositional framework for modeling multi-agent tasks DESIRE is introduced here. The following aspects are modeled and specified: [15].

(1) a task (de)composition, (2) information exchange, (3) sequencing of (sub)tasks, (4) subtask delegation, (5) knowledge structures. Information required/produced by a (sub)task is defined by input and output signatures of a component. The signatures used to name the information are defined in a predicate logic with a hierarchically ordered sort structure (order-sorted predicate logic). Units of information are represented by the ground atoms defined in the signature. The role information plays within reasoning is indicated by the level of an atom within a signature: different (meta) levels may be

distinguished. In a two-level situation, the lowest level is termed object-level information, and the second level meta-level information. Some specifics and a mathematical basis to such models with agent signatures might be obtained.

Meta-level information contains information about object-level information and reasoning processes; for example, for which atoms the values are still unknown (epistemic information). Similarly, tasks that include reasoning about other tasks are modeled as meta-level tasks with respect to object-level tasks. Often more than two levels of information and reasoning occur, resulting in meta-meta-information and reasoning. Information exchange between tasks is specified as information links between components. Each information link relates output of one component to input of another, by specifying which truth-value of a specific output atom is linked with which truth value of a specific input atom. For a multi-agent object information exchange model, see, for example [32].

5.2 Multitier Business Models

From e.g. (Nourani 2012) Presentation Layer o Runs with the address space if one or more web servers. Business Logic layer Runs with the address space of one or more application servers, and a Backend and DataBase layer.

The presentation layer contains components dealing with user interfaces and user interaction. Example a visual JAVA standalone application. A business logic layer contains components that work together to solve business problems. The components can be high-performance engines. Data layer is used by the business logic layer to persist state permanently. Control of the data layer is one or more databases that home the standalone. From an example content processing prototype (Nourani 2007, [2]) we can glimpse on the applications for the above section. A basic keyed database view provides the presentation of the model. It is the look of presentation of the model. It is the look of the application. We apply predefined user know functions on the view to present the applications look. The view should be notified when changes to the model.

The business logic updates the state of the model and helps control the flow of the application. With Struts, this is done with an Action class as a thin wrapper to the actual business logic. The model represents the world model for the actual business state of the application. The business objects update the application state application. The business objects update the Ap. Action Form bean represents the Model state at a session or request level, bean represents the Model state at a session or request level, and not at a persistent level. The JSP file reads information from the ActionForm bean using JSP tags. Our design applies the same functions that are presented on the that are the view for specific application to generate a content model for specific applications.

6 Augmented Learning and Knowledge Management

6.1 Augmented Learning with Smart Data

Competitive model planning above selects big data segments spanning infinite data. Possible big data is encoded on model diagrams with nondeterminism minimizing data segment spans. Big Data has a big value, it also takes organizations big effort to manage well and an effective governance discipline can fulfill its purpose. The Big Data Exponentials: Content, Apps: Consumers have been pledging their love for data visualizations for a while now, and data mining with multimedia discovery is the area being explored. Big data is a popular term used to describe the exponential growth and availability of data, both structured and unstructured. More accurate analyses may lead to more confident decision making. And better decisions can mean greater operational efficiencies, cost reductions, and reduced risk. Our novel techniques apply non-deterministic data model diagram filters to span big data spaces. Smart data is big data turned into actionable data that is available in real-time. Smart Data: What Purpose, Users, Processes, Platform. Users with data analysis, IT and marketing knowledge, can define processes, enabling processes to take advantage of smart data analytics platforms that can be deployed for the benefits of SmartData: efficiently scalable over many marketing processes. With smart data, we focus on valuable data and often smaller data sets that can be turned into actionable data and effective outcomes to address customer and business challenges. On our decision tree spanning techniques (Nourani and CBS group: [28]) a specific cooperating group "wins" to satisfy a goal, the agent group is presenting a model consistent with an intended world model for that goal. The value of big data is only multiplied by good data governance. Our techniques are in part ana-logical augmented learning applied to model discovery and data management. Eric Klopfer on an MIT press book 2011 describes the largely untapped potential of mobile learning Klopfer argues that the strengths of the mobile platform—its portability, context sensitivity, connectivity, and ubiquity—make it ideal for learning in schools. These games—either participatory (which require interaction with other players) or augmented reality (which augment the real world with virtual information. Our data modeling and discovery techniques apply competitive model diagrams with cooper-ating learning agents acting on game trees to manage knowledge.

6.2 Competitive Model Learning Heuristics

The first author had developed free proof tree techniques since projects at TU Berlin, 1994. Free proof trees allow us to carry on Skolemized tress on game tree computing models, for example, that can have unassigned variables. The techniques allow us to carry on predictive model diagrams realized on plans with free proof trees (Nourani 1994–2007). Thus essentially the basic heuristics here are satisfying nodes on agent AND/OR game trees. The general heuristics to accomplish that is a game tree deductive technique based on computing game tree unfoldings projected onto predictive model diagrams. Newer areas are on a volume chapter ([39], editor), for example [21] on impact competitive decision tree models. The soundness and completeness of these techniques, e.g., heuristics as a computing logic are published since [32] at several events e.g. AISB 1995, and Systems and Cybernetics (2005), [16]. In computer sci-ence, specifically in algorithms related to pathfinding, a heuristic function is said to be admissible if it never overestimates the cost of reaching the goal, i.e. the cost it estimates to reach the goal is not higher than the lowest possible cost from the current point in the path [1]. An admissible heuristic is also known as an optimistic heuristic.

An admissible heuristic is used to estimate the cost of reaching the goal state in an informed search algorithm. The heuristic nomenclature indicates that a heuristic function is called an admissible-heuristic if it never overestimates the cost of reaching the goal, i.e. the cost it estimates to reach the goal is not higher than the lowest possible cost from the current point in the path. An admissible heuristic is also known as an optimistic heuristic (Russell and Norvig 2002). We shall use the term optimistic heuristic from now on to save ambiguity with admissible sets from mathematics, e.g. first author's publications on descriptive computing, for the time being. What is the cost estimate on satisfying a goal on an unfolding projection to model diagrams, for example with SLNDF, to satisfy a goal? Our heuristics are based on satisfying nondeterministic Skolemized trees. The heuristics aim to decrease the unknown assignments on the trees. Since at least one path on the tree must have all assignments defined to T or F, and at most one such assignment closes the search, the "cost estimate," is no more than the lowest. To become more specific how game tree node degrees can be ranked, we state one example linear measure proposition since (Nourani-Schulte 2015). That was further extrapolated for big data heuristics in (Nourani-Fähndrich 2017). The big Data Sparse Heuristics, e.g. (Nourani 2016; Nourani-Fähndrich 2017: TU Berlin) agent state vectors are spanning with models for diagram values that either, true, false, or X-undetermined. The cross product with the model diagram for vectors is a matrix. That matrix is sparse coding to bigdata with the X's sparsing the matrix (Nourani 1992, ScandinviaAI), thus minimizing reaches for bigdata: hence sparse heuristics are entailed.

7 Conclusions

New bases for augmented model decision techniques with splitting decision tree for enterprise modeling and business planning with predictive analytics models were presented. Decision tree applications to analytics towards designing cognitive augmented business interfaces with applications to social media were presented. Augmented reasoning on business systems reflect on the innovation ecosystems. Data filtering is applied with function keyed knowledge bases for goal satisfiability with competitive business models coupled with predictive analytics models accomplish goals on business models. Spanning trees focus on plan goal models that can be processed on a vector state machine coupled with database preprocessor interfaces. Cognitive views and augmented models with heuristics on predictive analytics are developed based on ranked game trees from the first authors preceding publications on economic games and big data towards newer applications to decision tree heuristics. Newer areas on predictive analytics and impact competitive models are on an edited volume ([39], editor).

References

1. Breiman, L., Friedman, J.H., Olshen, R.A., Stone, C.J.: Classification and Regression Trees. Chapman & Hall (Wadsworth, Inc.), New York (1984)
2. Nourani, C.F.: W-interfaces, business intelligence, and content processing. In: Invited Industry Track Keynote, IAT-Intelligent Agent Technology, Atlanta, November 2013

3. Nourani, C.: Intelligent tree computing, decision trees and soft OOP tree computing. In: Frontiers in Soft Computing and Decision Systems Papers from the 1997 Fall Symposium, Boston   Technical Report FS-97-04 AAAI (1997). www.aaai.org/Press/Reports/Symposia/Fall/fs-97-04.html Programming. ISBN 1-57735-079-0

4. Nourani, C.F., Lauth, C., Pedersen, R.U.: Agent planning models, and attention span – a preliminary. IAT, Atlanta, November 2013

5. Wooldridge, M., Jennings, N.R.: Agent theories, architectures, and languages: a survey. In: Wooldridge, M., Jennings, N.R. (eds.) Intelligent Agents - Intelligent Multimedia New Computing Techniques, Design Paradigms, and Applications, pp. 51–92 (1999)

6. Nourani, C.F.: Model discovery for knowledge management. In: AAAI Workshop on Agent-Based Systems in the Business Context, Orlando, Florida, July 1999. AAAI Press, June 1998

7. Annosi, M.C., Brunetta, F., Magnusson, M.: Self-organizing coordination and control approach: the impact of social norms and self-regulated innovations activities in self-managed teams. In: Nourani, C. (ed.) Ecosystems and Technology: Idea Generation and Content Model Processing, chap. 3, edited volume. Apple Academic Press, Canada (2017)

8. Nourani, C.F.: Model discovery, intelligent W-Interfaces, and business intelligence with multitier designs. In: CollECTeR LatAm 2004, Santiago, Chile, 13–15 October 2004 (2004).   http://ing.utalca.cl/collecter/techsession.php

9. Nourani, C.F.: Competitive Models and Game Tree Planning, November 1999. Applications to Economic Games. A version published at SSGRR, L'Auquila, Rome, Itlay, September 2001 (2001)

10. Nourani, C.F.: Business planning and cross-organizational models. In: Workshop on Collaborative Cross-Organisational Process Design, Linz, Austria, September 2005. http://www.mensch-und-computer.de/mc2005

11. Schönberger, H.: Systematic spin-off processes in university-industry ecosystem. In: Cleyn, S.H.D., Festel, G. (eds.) Academic Spinn-offs and Technology Transfer in Europe: Best Practices and Breakthrough Models, pp. 93–107. Elgar Publishing Ltd., Chellenham UK and Northhampton US (2016)

12. Nourani, C.F., Schulte, O.: Multiplayer games, competitive models, descriptive computing. In: EUROPMENT Conference Computers, Automatic Control, Signal Processing and Systems Science (2014). ISBN 978-1-61804-233-0

13. Brazier, F.M.T., Jonker, C.M., Treur, J.: Formalisation of a cooperation model based on joint intentions. In: Müller, J.P., Wooldridge, M.J., Jennings, N.R. (eds.) ATAL 1996. LNCS, vol. 1193, pp. 141–155. Springer, Heidelberg (1997). https://doi.org/10.1007/BFb0013583

14. Nourani, C.F., Fähndrich, J.: A formal approach to agent planning with inference trees. NAEC, Trieste, August 2015

15. Brazier, F.M.T., Dunin-Keplicz, B.M., Jennings, N.R., Treur, J.: DESIRE: modeling multi-agent systems in a compositional formal framework. Int. J. Coop. Inf. Syst. 6(1), 67–94 (1997)

16. Nourani, C.F.: A predictive tableaux visual analytics, Slovakia. In: ICTIC - Proceedings in Conference of Informatics and Management Sciences, vol. 4, issue 1, March 2015. EDIS - Publishing Institution of the University of Zilina Powered by Thomson, Slovakia (2015). ISSN 1339-9144, CD ROM ISSN 1339-231X. ISBN 978-80-554-1002-9

17. Lauth, C., Vestergaard, L., Blom, R., Bajrovic, S., Marcynova, M.W., Pedersen, R.U.: 155GATESENSE – Making Sense of Massive Open Data Resources into Sustainable Business Solutions. Copenhagen Business School, IT Management Department

18. Nourani, C.F., Fähndrich, J.: Decisions, inference trees, and big data heuristics in computing predictive analytics, business intelligence, and economics modeling techniques with start-ups and incubators. Hardcover Taylor & Francis (2018). ISBN 978-1

19. Underwood, J.: IBM cognitive analytics overview (2019)
20. Bullard, J., Duffy, J.: A model of learning and emulation with artificial adaptive agents. J. Econ. Dyn. Control **22**(2), 179–207 (1998)
21. Nourani, C.F., Lauth, C.: Strategic decision trees on impact competitive models. In: Predictive Analytics and Economics. Apple Academic Press (2018)
22. Genesereth, M.R., Nilsson, N.J.: Logical Foundations of Artificial Intelligence. Morgan-Kaufmann, Burlington (1987)
23. Nourani, C.F.: Game Trees, Competitive Models, and ERP, New Business Models and Enabling Technologies. Management School, St Petersburg, Russia, Keynote Address, June 2002. Fraunhofer Institute for Open Communication Systems, Germany. Proceedings Editor Nikolai Krivulin (2002)
24. Huhns, M., Singh, M.P.: Cognitive agents. In: IEEE Internet Computing (1998)
25. Kinny, D., Georgeff, M., Rao, A.: A methodology and modelling technique for systems of BDI agents. In: Van de Velde, W., Perram, J.W. (eds.) MAAMAW 1996. LNCS, vol. 1038, pp. 56–71. Springer, Heidelberg (1996). https://doi.org/10.1007/BFb0031846
26. Lauth, C., Berendt, B., Pfleging, B., Schmidt, A.: Ubiquitous computing. In: Mehler, A.L., Romary, L. (eds.) Handbook of Technical Communication. Walter de Gruyter (2012)
27. Nourani, C.F., Schulte, O.: Multiagent decision trees, competitive models, and goal satisfiability. In: DICTAP, Ostrava, Czech Republic, July 2013
28. Nourani, C.F., Lauth, C., Pedersen, R.U.: Merging process-oriented ontologies with cognitive agent, planning and attention spanning. Open J. Bus. Model Innov. (2015). https://sustainablebusinessmodel.org/2015/01/23/new-journal-open-journal-of-business-model-innovation/
29. Moore, R.C.: Reasoning about knowledge and action. In: AI Center Technical Note 191, SRI International Menlo Park, California (1980)
30. Nourani, C.F.: Planning and plausible reasoning in artificial intelligence, diagrams, planning, and reasoning. In: Proceedings of Scandinavian Conference on Artificial Intelligence, Denmark, IOS Press (1991)
31. Nourani, C.F., Hoppe, Th.: GF-Diagrams for models and free proof trees. In: Proceedings the Berlin Logic Colloquium, Humboldt University, Mathematics Department, May 1994
32. Nourani, C.F.: Slalom tree computing - a computing theory for artificial intelligence, June 1994. Revised in A.I. Commun. **9**(4), December 1996, IOS Press
33. Pedersen, R.U.: Micro information systems and ubiquitous knowledge discovery. In: May, M., Saitta, L. (eds.) Ubiquitous Knowledge Discovery. LNCS (LNAI), vol. 6202, pp. 216–234. Springer, Heidelberg (2010). https://doi.org/10.1007/978-3-642-16392-0_13
34. Nourani, C.F., Loo, G.S.L.: KR and model discovery from active DB with predictive logic. The University of Auckland MSIS, New Zealand International Conference on Business and Financial Applications of Data Mining, Cambridge University, England, August 2000 (1998)
35. Nourani, C.F.: Competitive models augmented learning and big data filtering heuristics. In: IJCCAI Stokholm, 6th AI4KM 2018: AI-Based Innovation in Digital Services, 15 July 2018 (2018)
36. Rao, A.S., Georgeff, M.P.: Modeling rational agents within a BID-architecture. In: Fikes, R., Sandewall, E. (eds.) Proceedings of the Second Conference on Knowledge (1991)
37. Nourani, C.F.: Business modeling and forecasting. In: AIEC-AAAI 1999, Orlando, July 1999. AAAI Press, November 1998
38. Nourani, C.F.: Intelligent Multimedia Computer Science - Business Interfaces, Wireless Computing, Databases and Data Mining. American Scientific and Publishers (2005). http://www.aspbs.com/multimedia.htmlDecember2004
39. Cyrus, N.F.: Computing Predictive Analytics, Business Intelligence and Economics. Apple Academic Press, Francis (2018)

40. Nourani, C.F.: Business planning and cross-organizational models. In: Workshop on Collaborative Cross-Organisational Process Design, Linz, Austria (2005). http://www. mensch-und-computer.de/mc2005
41. Mercier-Laurent, E.: Innovation eco-systems and technology. In: Nourani, C. (ed.) Ecosystems and Technology: Idea Generation and Content Model Processing, chap. 2, edited volume. Apple Academic Press, Canada (2015)
42. Nourani, C.F.: Multiagent games, competitive models, and game tree planning. In: Fall Symposium, Intent Inference. AAAI Press, Boston (2002)
43. Nourani, C.F., Schulte, O.: Multiagent Games, Competitive Models, Descriptive Computing SFU, Vancouver, Canada Draft February 2011, Revision 1: 25 September 2012 SFU, Vancouver, Canada Computation Logic Lab. EUROPMENT, April 2014, Prague (2014)

AI Classification in Collaboration for Innovation of Electric Motors of Household Appliances

Asuman Firat[1] and Gulgun Kayakutlu[2(✉)]

[1] Washing Machine Plant R&D, Arcelik, Tuzla, Istanbul, Turkey
asuman.firat@arcelik.com
[2] Istanbul Technical University Energy Institute, Maslak, Istanbul, Turkey
gkayakutlu@gmail.com

Abstract. Electric motors are important components of household appliance that effects the energy efficiency and noise level with a social impact. Considering the evolution period of electric motors in household appliances, innovation can be seen at the end of each life cycle of motor technology for every single product. Therefore, it can be stated that electric motors are open for innovation. There are several ways for innovation. Collaboration is one of them. Recently, improvement in sharing economies also resulted with knowledge sharing due to shortage of resources. In order to achieve efficiency with limited sources collaboration is essential. However, collaborating partner is very important to get successful results. Unfortunately there are lots of examples that collaboration ends up without any beneficial. As a result of evaluation of previous studies and experiences, expert knowledge is established. Classification method based on expert knowledge is chosen to give the decision of collaboration for each candidate corporation. Artificial intelligence is used for this critical decision making.

Keywords: Innovation · Collaboration · Classification

1 Introduction

Since 19th century electric motors are very popular in the industry thanks to important scientists such as Faraday, Oersted, Tesla, etc. for their innovative solutions. Electric motors are the machines that converts electrical energy to the mechanical energy. Mechanical energy is used so many areas that needs rotational movement and torque. Pumps, household appliances, elevators, conveyors are some of the examples of these application areas.

Previously most of applications used the motors whose input is other energies than electricity. Motors that convert chemical energy to the mechanical energy lose their importance day by day. Since they use petroleum, they increase dependence on those countries who have this source. On the other hand, there are many resources to create electricity. Recent technologies give us chance to use natural resources such as sun and wind to obtain electrical energy, in order not to give harm to the nature.

© IFIP International Federation for Information Processing 2020
Published by Springer Nature Switzerland AG 2020
E. Mercier-Laurent (Ed.): AI4KM 2018, IFIP AICT 588, pp. 107–123, 2020.
https://doi.org/10.1007/978-3-030-52903-1_9

Additionally, electric motors have such advantages like higher efficiency and silent working conditions. Due to limited resources of energy and shortage that is not far from today's world, efficiency is very important. Although there is a big history in conventional motors of vehicles, number of electric vehicles are increasing so that efficiency and silence advantages are given to the drivers.

1.1 Innovation of Electric Motors in Household Appliances

Most of the electric consumer appliances in a house are washing machines, dries, dishwashers and refrigerators. There are plenty of houses with these appliances, therefore electric motors are inside of the houses. As technology level increases, requirements from these appliances also changes. In ancient times, for example an idea of a machine that is washing clothes was so surprising for the people. On the other hand, nowadays energy level of a washing machine is very important argument for the people who buys it. Such development is also valid for other appliances.

Considering washing machines, there are two main operating points in motor point of view. One of them is washing period that is slow rotation with large torque requirement. The other one is spinning period that is high speed rotation with low torque requirement.

In order to satisfy these requirements induction motors were used. These motors are controlled via a big electronic card so that this two different operating condition is satisfied. However big electronic card and big motor couple were expensive. Due to these expensive parts, washing machine was also expensive and this was not the case people prefer.

Afterwards, universal motors are started to be used. Good news about this type of motor is that universal motors are plug-in motors. Only a few electronic component is needed in order to control two opposite operating point of the washing machine. On the other hand, disadvantage of this motor is that brushes that are used in these motors for commutation. Brushes are carbon structures and due to friction during operation, brushes wear down. This disadvantage results in lower life cycle of the motor and so that washing machine. Since customers want to use their washing machine more than 10 years, the need for innovation in motor technology is raised. Another disadvantage of this motor is that friction of brushes increases noise level of washing machine.

Due to the problems created by brushes, new motor technologies such as brushless motors became popular. One of them was direct drive motors that were so popular in that time period which is beginning of 2000's. These motors were directly mounted on the drum without any brush structure within the motor. Thanks to the permanent magnet technology included in direct drive motor, efficiency of these motors were higher than universal motors. Patents about permanent magnet usage limited motor applications until these years. Direct drive motor also used big electronic card in order to control operations of the motor. Although this solution was not the cheapest solution, it offered long-life and noiseless washing machines. Added to its cost problem, direct drive motor assembly to the washing machine was so precise operation that is open to some faults coming from human operators.

About five years later a permanent magnet motor is designed by using an existing motor with minimum investment. Operation control is done by a big electronic card.

This motor was assembled to the washing machine by belt-pulley system so that minimizing production problems. It also had long life time and noiseless structure. However, this motor and electronic driver system was not as cheap as universal motor system.

At that point new target was to have a motor system that has the same cost with universal motor system. Thanks to new technology coming from winding machines that is used in motor production, it was applicable to cancel some of the windings that are not used during operation of the motor. In other words, innovation came with simplification. Additionally, magnets are arranged so that their benefits are increased. Moreover, electronic driver technology continued to develop. As a result of it more capable drivers with cheaper components are available.

Finally washing machines can provide long life, noiseless and higher energy efficiency with reasonable prices. A brief illustration that shows this development period is given in Fig. 1.

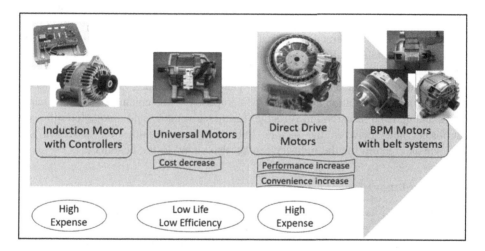

Fig. 1. Development period of washing machine motors

Considering all period; many innovation types are easily observed. Each type of the motor is examples of product innovation. Step from induction motor to universal motor includes physical characteristic change. Direct drive motors have different architecture form universal motors. Direct drive motors and Brushless Permanent Magnet (BPM) with belt systems are modular innovation. Since they include both change in subsystem and change in linkages between subsystems washing machines are clearly different between each other.

Motor technology development of dishwasher, drier and refrigerator was not so complicated. These machines have one operating conditions. Therefore, simple induction motor types without electronic control were used in these appliances. On the other hand, in order to increase efficiency of these appliances, control of the motor is necessary. Permanent magnet motors are also used in these appliances for efficiency and controllability. For these appliances controllability provides low noise requirement too.

Additionally, customer expectations did not end up. Requirements that are related with motor of the household appliances are lower noise, higher efficiency with lower cost. In other words innovation is needed in this area to achieve these challenges.

2 Innovation

It is clear that in order to improve economy of a country for improving competitiveness, intellectual capital and innovation capability are two important parameters. Innovation is an invention that brings improvement together with money. Innovation is a road from ideas to values that someone prefers to pay for. A product or a process can be innovative. It starts from idea creation by means of lots of techniques. Experimentation is the second step.

Universities are considered to be necessary for innovation for the subjects coming from production areas. Thus academic-industry collaboration is established mostly. Universities and research institutes are the major drivers of scientific and technological advancement. However, technology breakthroughs cannot become an innovation until it is successfully commercialized. That is why university-industry collaboration is important. The intellectual resources continuously provided by university are a priceless intangible asset to a company [7].

Academic-industrial partnerships have gains for both sides: intellectual property generation and exploitation for industrial competitiveness, enhanced research capabilities and updated research infrastructure for the universities and innovation diffusion that fosters links between the sectors. Publication opportunities for academia and employment creation for the industry can be also added to the benefits [1].

2.1 Open Innovation

Open innovation is driven by a desire to realize: cost reduction for technology development, reduced risk for market entry, to achieve economies of scale for production, reduce lead times for product or service development, and to promote shared learning. In essence the ability to "tap into shared creativity is a considerable driver in the open innovation context and this creates the motivation for organizations to link with other organizations as they no longer have to make or source everything themselves. With the introduction of collaborate into traditional decisions of make or buy a company can extend its capabilities in interaction with others [5].

In today's global society, firms recognize they have much to gain from creating partnerships and engaging with the rest of the world. Open innovation refers to how organizations use internal and external sourcing and markets paths for innovation, or share innovation processes. Open innovation is recognized as a progression from the classical linear models of innovation, from technology-push, through supply-chains, to network or collaboration focused innovation. For example, in 2007 a number of organizations working in the IT industry came together to create the Open Handset Alliance and later to launch the globally successful "Android" operating system and software platform. The organizations included Samsung, Intel and Qualcom (handset and component manufacturers); Google (a software developer) and T-Mobile (a mobile telephone operator) who loosely followed a vertical integration (or supply-chain) derived structure. This is a well versed example of open innovation around a multi-player venture that could be argued to be market driven-the needs of the customers (or users) creating the motivation for user-led innovation. Other examples indicate how firms may collaborate on horizontal level, in terms of complementary (co-operation) and competing organizations (co-opetition), such as the "Ecomagination" initiative that led General Electrics to collaborate with a range of smaller and less-established organizations to create emergent "green technology" solutions and the development activity between Sony, Samsung and a number of other high-tech electronics companies which enabled them to develop core technology that was then sold by each organization in competition with its collaborators [5].

2.2 Innovation Ecosystem

An innovation ecosystem allows firms to create value that no single firm could create alone. The health and performance of each firm is dependent on the health and performance of the whole. Therefore, the competition is not limited to company to company, instead the competition takes places from ecosystem to ecosystem. An innovation ecosystem is a place where innovative enterprises can integrate resources and realize innovation.

The competition among innovative enterprises has shifted from their products and services to the innovation ecosystems they belong to. It is hard for a single firm to have all the elements required for successful innovation. Companies should cooperate with suppliers, outsourcers, distributors, intermediary agents, customers, research institutes, universities, and governments closely, and take full consideration of the interdependences between components and complements, to construct a healthy innovation ecosystem, and provide valuable products and services to their customers. Many companies are trying to build or join a vigorous innovation ecosystem in order to enhance their capabilities toward innovation and their market responses. Successful innovation usually depends on close collaboration among firms and their partners [7].

An innovation ecosystem (Fig. 2) is the complex relationships that are formed between actors or entities whose functional goal is to enable technology development and innovation. The actors include the material resources (funds, equipment, facilities, etc.) and the human capital (students, faculty, staff, industry researchers, industry representatives, etc.) that make up the institutional entities participating in the ecosystem (universities, colleges of engineering, business schools, business firms, venture capitalists, industry-university research institutes, federal or industrial supported centers of excellence, state and/or local economic development and business assistance organizations, funding agencies, policy makers, etc.). There exists a lot of material, energy, and information exchanges within an ecosystem and between the ecosystem and the environment, which help maintain the stability and efficiency of the ecosystem.

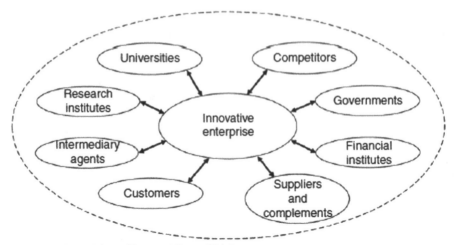

Source: Adapted from Zhao and Zeng (2014)

Fig. 2. Innovation ecosystem

In innovation ecosystems, companies can adopt a coopetition strategy: they compete in gaining market share, but cooperate for defense, development and growing of their ecosystems at the same time. A single organization may participate in several linked ecosystems, and may have different roles in each. Companies such as Apple, IBM, Ford, and Walmart are regarded as leaders of innovation ecosystems and perform a critical role in enhancing innovation and productivity. They strategically nurture their innovation ecosystems by investing in innovation partners that help make their suppliers, customers, and other members of their ecosystem smarter, faster, richer, more innovative, and more creative. The core company that plays a central role in the innovation ecosystem is valued by all of the rest of the ecosystem. Other members can utilize the abilities of the ecosystem such as services, tools or technologies to enhance their own innovation performance as well as adding value to the ecosystem by providing new applications and complementary products [7].

3 Collaboration

On 25th September of 2015, United Nations accepted 17 Goals to transform our world that is called Sustainable Development Goals. Sustainable development agenda includes goals such as zero hunger, end of the poverty, gender equality ... etc. (Fig. 3).

Most of the global companies included these goals as their own development goals. In case these goals are achieved, national revenue of all world will increase dramatically. Sustainability will provide companies respectfulness and trust. As a result of it, its customers, investors and human resources will increase. According to Better Business Better World report (a call to action to business leaders to align with the

Fig. 3. Sustainable development goals accepted in 2015 by United Nations

Sustainable Development Goals); six action is listed for companies in order to let them to be leader in sustainable development. Two of these actions are related with collaborations.

1. Collaborate with other companies in your sector to transfer global transformation to all sustainable market.
2. Collaborate with government, civil society and regulations so that provide all natural sources to be priced transparently and provide human resources to be priced fairly.

Companies that can optimize their resource usage will be in a better position than the others. Humans are existing for each other. Therefore, in future, collaboration will be more important than past. Leaders of future will be determined by their collaboration competency [2].

The road that goes to perfect collaboration is given in Fig. 4.

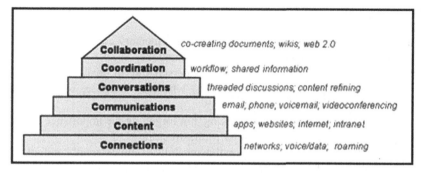

Fig. 4. Roadmap for perfect collaboration

Like any pyramid, the bottom layers provide essential foundations for those above. The diagram illustrates the 6Cs of collaboration:

- Connections. Before collaboration can start, the participants must connect with each other, irrespective of location. Good high bandwidth networks are an essential prerequisite in this day and age.
- Content. Explicit content is usually an input and output of collaboration. Documents and databases, accessible through web-based portals are prominent in this layer.
- Communications. Much collaborative work takes place through personal communications and conversation. This layer includes both voice and data communications. It also covers a variety of communications patterns, ranging from one-to-one, one-to-many and many-to-many.
- Conversations. Conversations are sequences of communications. This layer adds the much overlooked function of orchestrating and recording the essence of conversations in a reusable way.
- Coordination. At this layer, a systematic approach is involved to ensure that functions at lower layers, such as content sharing and conversations, "function together or occupy their proper place as parts of an interrelated whole".
- Collaboration. This layer represents the highest level of collaboration capability. Each piece of work, however large or small, is done in a collaborative way. Key features at this level are a collaborative style of working and technology tools to match.

(For completeness, there is a 7C version which includes as the second layer Computation - for computer-computer collaboration without human intervention.)

Transformation as a technology network requires collaborative networks including all business units, joint ventures and R&D Centers. With a wider aspect, universities, other companies, national labs, information systems and legal advisers are part of this ecology. Collaborative networks result in new discoveries with saved time and çosts. In order to get success from this system the following six key aspects should be considered well.

- Strategic selection of project - selecting the development method (such as acquisition, in-house or partnership) based on a business-competitive strength matrix.
- Selecting partners based on key criteria - world class competency, commitment, trust etc.
- Matching projects and partners - meshing complementary competencies, matching interests, and in general creating a win-win situation.
- Effective project management, with clear understanding of goals.
- A strong co-manager (business champion) who sets the pace, respects cultural diversity and has high credibility.
- Effective communications and networking, not forgetting the importance of face-to-face communications and local support infrastructures.
- Shift from a competitive to a collaborative mentality, both externally and internally.
- Proper protection of intellectual property when knowledge is shared more freely; preventing leakage of vital knowledge.
- Capable of working across different cultures, both company and national.

- Entry and exit strategies for collaborations should be clearly identified.
- Exactly determination of boundaries between companies and between employees, contractors, suppliers and partners.

Especially R&D Managers have to move much further if their companies are to be leaders in innovation [6]. The role of the orchestrator requires the ability to collaborate with several partners simultaneously, while not having direct control, and the skills of complex project management. It is clear that government regulations have a strong influence on innovation at the national, regional and company levels [7].

3.1 Collaboration in Innovation

Economic competitiveness capability depends on capital, export, infrastructure, competences/skill and process & technology. "Technology" and "skills" dimensions are two main dimensions contributing to play a significant role in enhancing the RD capacity. Knowledge creation, technology diffusion and development of R&D should be attracted from the biggest countries. Building industrial capabilities requires technology cooperation between local and international companies, government and research/education institutions [9].

Technological innovation is the driving force for the development of electric motors. At each time period of change, competitors are waiting just behind to get more share in the market. Sustainable innovation is needed to continue the business. This is valid for all industrial sectors such as electrical vehicles. Since their aim is also lower energy consumption, it is understandable to check their way of innovation. Innovation method differs between companies in the meaning of ecological environment, market positioning, innovation path and business model. For example, Toyota made optimized configuration in the global and built enterprise ecosystem to make progressive disruptive innovation and develop the middle and low-end market. Toyota created a good innovation environment by the way of cooperating with local universities, enterprises and research institutes in various regions. On the other hand, Tesla being in a technology innovation environment preferred quick disruptive innovation for high-end market. Tesla like to stand in the preface to the era of early adaptors. In order to promote the development of electric vehicle technology, Tesla shared all the Tesla's patented technology with other companies. As a result, it promoted the development of electric vehicle industry innovation environment. Additionally, BYD a company in Shenzen, formed a plurality of core technologies through cooperation with domestic and foreign for niche-based market. BYD cooperated with the United States, Chrysler and other international giants such as Daimler-Benz and Intel, to further enhance its technical level and international brand influence [4].

It is notable that for industrial partners just in time information is a major requirement. Industrial communities often follow the money and cannot be sustained without the financial benefits received. Here, other benefits need to be built into the model to ensure sustainability of the cluster and ongoing interest in the communities. The supply of skilled workers and specialized facilities has a draw for new companies and can be a magnet for growth, many lessons remain for how academic and industrial communities can interwork and co-relate best practices [1].

During research and development activities of electric motors, many other partners contributed to the design stage of the motor. Requirements are collected from different customers. Additionally, regulations also determine the limitations of the designs. Both of them determine specifications of the design. It is clear that heart of the innovation comes from material, production equipment or design. Suppliers of motor producers can be either component supplier or equipment supplier. Both of them have some advantages as they work with different types of companies. Therefore, they give different aspects to achieve design targets. In some stages competitors also offer different motor designs. They also contributed innovation of the motor by showing advantages and disadvantages of some design types. Istanbul Technical University performed magnetic and mechanical analysis about different configurations of new motor designs. Several researches from different Universities of all over the world are studied deeply Fig. 5.

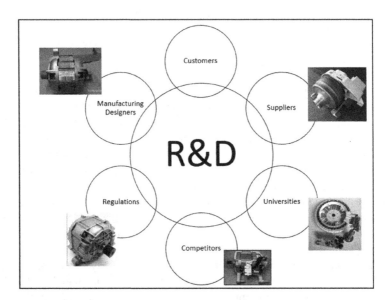

Fig. 5. Collaboration in innovation

All of these collaborations will also lead to achieve better and better designs. Many types of transformations of knowledge can be obtained from each of these collaborations. Such innovation will lead to competency advantage and increase in revenue.

3.2 Collaborative Innovation in Turkey

According to European statistics database Eurostat, collaborative innovation in Turkey is given in following charts (Figs. 6 and 7).

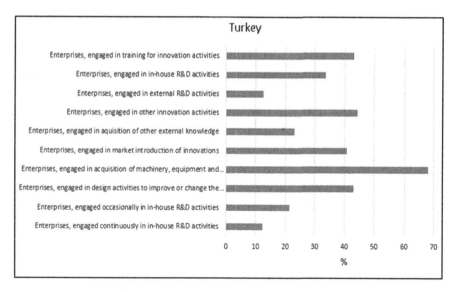

Fig. 6. Innovation ways in Turkey

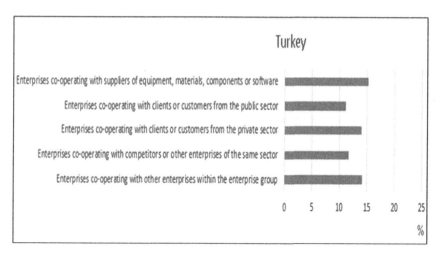

Fig. 7. Turkey cooperation distribution

As can be seen from the graphics, percentage of collaboration with suppliers in Turkey very low. Private sector is more preferred partner compared to public sector partner. Enterprises prefer to collaborate with other enterprises rather than competitors.

It is clear that Turkey should increase collaboration competency in order to be one of the most innovative countries.

3.3   Parameters Effecting Collaboration Quality

Unfortunately, some of the collaborations end up with failure. Studies have shown that between 30% and 70% of alliances fail; in other words; they neither meet the goals of their parent companies nor deliver on the operational or strategic benefits [3]. Many reasons can be listed for this failure. Companies prefer to sign contract in order to prevent failure. However, in case structure of the candidate is not suitable for the collaboration; contract will not solve the problem. As a result of it money and time is spent and the amount is depending on importance of the project.

There are many parameters that have impact on collaboration quality. Referring study done by Worasinchai and Bechina [9], many techniques used to determine parameters that effects collaboration quality. Lots of surveys, interviews were conducted with different managers from both sides of collaboration units in order to formulate parameters to understand the knowledge flow and the learning processes between foreign companies and local Universities.

Additionally, experience from a Turkish Well-known R&D Center is also evaluated for collaboration quality. Although effectiveness of some of the parameters differ according to implicit and explicit knowledge, the difference is not considered to determine collaboration quality.

- Corporations that are collaborated previously has good impact in collaboration decisions.
- Collaboration with supplier has positive impact.
- Collaboration with a corporation from private sector brings better result than a corporation from public sector.
- Although according to some sectors collaboration with a competitor has a positive impact, it has negative impact in collaboration with the aim of innovation.
- Collaboration with a corporation that has in-house R&D activities results with innovation.
- Corporations that has higher percentage of employers with university education creates good collaborations.
- Collaborations that has top executive decision power of all corporations increases the collaboration quality. Strong involvement of leadership in the decision making is crucial for a successful collaboration.
- Corporations from foreign countries, also local countries that spend many years on related subject increases collaboration quality.
- Corporations that have own R&D strategy are good choices for innovative collaborations. The intensiveness of R&D strategy has a positive effect on the intention to share knowledge.
- Most of the companies do not want to share confidential information. Because protection of knowledge seen as having a competitive advantage to the corporations. The clear lack of an intellectual property strategy makes the companies quite often reluctant to involve outside people in their business routines or within the premises of the enterprise. Trust is seen as a fundamental core value. Therefore, as confidential information increases within collaboration, quality of the results decreases.
- Benefit level of all the companies should be as much as high for innovative collaborations. The level of benefits has a positive effect on the intention to share knowledge. Benefits should be clearly evaluated and highlighted in order to

promote stronger collaboration. The benefits as stated in the interviews are related to cost reduction, enhancing the skills of employees, gaining a better position in the market place, and so forth.

3.4   Classification and Constraint Programming for Collaboration

Knowledge engineering is a core part of artificial intelligence in research. Machines can often act and react like humans only if they have abundant information relating to the world. Artificial intelligence must have access to objects, categories, properties and relations between all of them to implement knowledge engineering. Initiating common sense, reasoning and problem-solving power in machines is a difficult and tedious task [8]. AI is mostly used to do this tedious task.

Selection of a collaboration partner may be subjective decision sometime. As a result of being human, decision maker may be effected from any other properties of corporation and leads to wrong judgment. Thus AI is used to give such decision. It should be also added; opposite to the general idea implying that AI will take place of human; the valuable output comes from collaboration of AI and common sense of human.

One of the advantages of AI is to speed up the process of decision making. Rules are listed and according to definitions, AI decides the best solution. Compared to human decisions, AI will prefer the most objective option, fastly.

In general, a classification includes following steps. Firstly, a set of data is collected. Observations are extracted from those data. Answer of a question is determined according to these observations. In case of machine learning new observations are added to the observations and answer of the question converging to the best solution (Fig. 8).

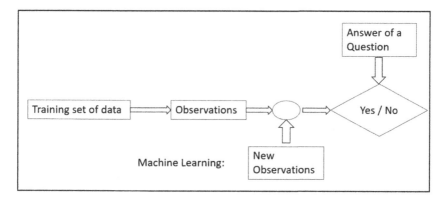

Fig. 8. Steps of a classification

Constraint programming is performed as shown in Fig. 9. Training set of data includes all the data of different corporations. Observations that are shown with colored boxes show the result of the collaboration quality.

Corporation		C1	C2	C3	C4	C5	C6	C7	C8	C9	C10	C11	C12	C13	C14	C15	C16	C17	C18	C19	C20
Is this the first time to collaborate with this Corporation?	[y/n?]	y	n	y	y	y	y	y	y	y	y	y	y	y	n	y	n	y	y	y	y
Is this corporation one of the supplier?	[y/n?]	n	n	y	n	n	n	n	n	n	y	y	y	y	y	y	n	n	y	y	y
Is this corporation University?	[y/n?]	y	y	y	y	y	y	y	y	y	y	y	y	y	y	y	y	y	y	y	y
Advisory/consultant	[y/n?]	y	n	n	n	n	n	n	n	n	y	y	y	y	y	y	y	n	n	y	y
Is the company local or from abroad?		local	local	local	local	local	abroad	local	local	local	local	local	local	local	local	local	local	local	local	local	local
Does the company have any relation with government policy?	[y/n?]	y	n	n	n	n	y	n	n	n	y	y	y	n	n	y	y	y	y	y	y
Is the company from Public or Private Sector?		private	private	public	public	private	private	private	public	private	public	private	private	private	private	private	private	private	private	private	private
Is the company one of the Competitors?	[y/n?]	y	n	n	n	n	n	n	n	y	y	y	y	y	y	y	y	y	y	y	y
Does the company have in-house R&D activity continuously?	[y/n?]	y	y	y	y	n	n	n	y	n	y	y	y	y	y	y	y	y	y	y	y
Percentage of employees that have university education		60%	80%	90%	100%	30%	95%	100%	100%	80%	90%	65%	85%	40%	83%	75%	70%	90%	80%	70%	90%
Top Executive Decision Power	[y/n?]	y	y	y	y	y	y	y	y	y	y	y	y	n	n	n	y	n	y	y	y
Years (Experience on corporation subject)			5	10	14	10	16	4	10	20	2	5	8	18	22	1	3	12	17	4	9
R&D Strategy	[y/n?]	y	y	n	y	n	y	y	n	y	y	y	y	n	n	y	y	y	y	y	y
Confidential Information	[y/n?]	y	y	y	y	n	y	y	y	n	y	y	y	n	y	y	n	n	n	y	y
Benefits Level	[y/n?]	y	y	y	y	y	y	y	y	y	y	y	y	y	y	y	y	y	y	y	y
Collaboration? [Yes/No]		Yes	Yes	Yes	Yes	Yes	No	Yes	Yes	No	No	Yes	Yes	Yes	Yes	No	No	Yes	Yes	Yes	Yes

Fig. 9. Training set of data and observations

As mentioned earlier; expert knowledge is used to determine collaboration parameters. Rules regarding these parameters are created and defined in a conditional programming environment such as Excel, Python, etc. Conditional statements check result of a parameter with a value. If the result is the same with the value, the action will be in one way. If the result is not the same with the value, the action will be in opposite way.

Question list (Table 1) also shows the parameters that effect collaboration quality. Certainly all of those questions do not have the same effect on collaboration quality. Therefore each question has its own weight. All answers with weighted values are summed to get a total score. According to expert knowledge limit score for good collaboration is 80. In case score is higher than 80, collaboration has high potential for good results.

Table 1. Question list

Weight	Questions	
	Corporation	
3	Is this the first time to collaborate with this corporation?	[y/n?]
1	Is this corporation one of the supplier?	[y/n?]
2	Is this corporation university?	[y/n?]
1	Advisers/consultant	[y/n?]
1	Is the company local or from abroad?	
1	Does the company have any relation with government policy?	[y/n?]
2	Is the company from public or private sector?	
1	Is the company one of the Competitors?	[y/n?]
2	Does the company have in-house R&D activity continuously?	[y/n?]
6	Percentage of employees that have university education	
15	Top executive decision power	[y/n?]
8	Years (experience on corporation subject)	
10	R&D strategy	[y/n?]
12	Confidential information	[y/n?]
8	Benefits level	[y/n?]

A new corporation or improved corporation is checked whether it is suitable or not for innovation subjects. Furthermore the list also shows improvement ways for better collaborations. Since this is the most objective solution, it also speeds up decision making process. As a result of this study, collaboration with 5 partner that has the highest score brought a motor design with given results (Fig. 10).

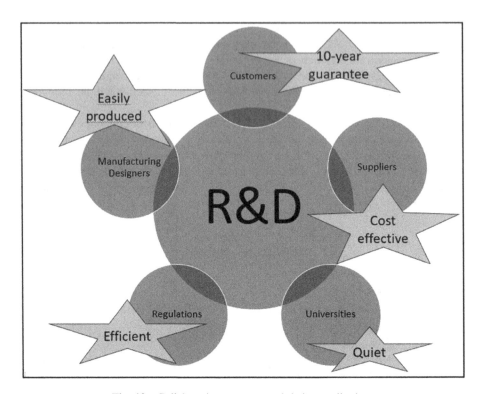

Fig. 10. Collaboration partners and their contributions

As a conclusion, innovation in electric motors will never end up. In order to get better results collaborative innovation has to be supported. This study classifies the success in collaborative innovation by constraint programming. Additionally other intelligent methods can be integrated to have dynamic solution. Behavioral models could improve decisions.

4   Conclusion

Energy that can be used by people is limited and quantity that can be used is decreasing day by day. There are some searches and studies for new energy resources. On the other hand, some group of people are working on efficient use of energy. Electric motors mounted on household appliances are one of the basic energy consumer that is used by many people all around the world. Therefore, in order to decrease energy consumption in houses electric motors are one of the components that should be considered.

In recent years' technology is the main component that brings money to the countries. All big countries try to develop products or services that have low weight with high values. Additionally, life cycle of these products are very short. Therefore, sustainability in innovation is mandatory. Popularity of sharing economies are increasing day by day in all areas. As a mirror of it knowledge sharing through good collaborations are necessary.

Due to shortages in resources collaboration is one of the tool for innovation. Borders are disappearing between people, companies or even countries with the help of worldwide web. As a result of it many technology developer company use collaborations in order to have the best product. Collaboration can be a way of innovation in order to solve a part of a big problem such as energy shortage. Thus efficient products with reasonable prices can be developed.

In this study first of all, innovation is described including open innovation. Importance of collaboration for innovation is described clearly. Afterwards parameters that effect collaboration quality are listed with the help of previous studies and R&D experiences. Moreover, a knowledge management method is suggested to choose the right corporation for better collaborations in order to get innovation. Considering the parameters, artificial intelligence classification is used in order to determine if a candidate is suitable for collaboration. Application of this method created 5 good collaboration. As a result of it, a motor with advantages of efficient, quiet, cost effective, easily produced and 10-year guarantee is designed.

Innovation in electric motors will continue, as it is clear from today's technology. The result will also get more beneficial with lower sources. Therefore in order to get better results collaborations also needed to have higher qualities. Future work for better collaborations may include to get more accurate answers from fewer questions. Additionally, it is clear that next future will be established with the help of collaborations. Therefore methods that define perfect collaborations will be on the table.

References

1. Freitas, S., Mayer, I., Arnab, S., Marshall, I.: Industrial and academic collaboration: hybrid models for research and innovation diffusion. J. High. Educ. Policy Manage. **36**(1), 2–14 (2014)
2. https://hbrturkiye.com/blog/surdurulebilir-kalkinma-liderligi. Accessed 25 Apr 2020
3. Kale, P., Singh, H.: Managing strategic alliances: what do we know now, and where do we go from here? Acad. Manag. Perspect. **23**(3), 45–62 (2009)
4. Liu, J., Meng, Z.: Innovation model analysis of new energy vehicles: taking Toyota, Tesla and BYD as an example. In: 13th Global Congress on Manufacturing and Management, GCMM (2016)
5. Öberg, C., Alexander, A.T.: The openness of open innovation in ecosystems – integrating innovation and management literature on knowledge linkages. J. Innov. Knowl. **4**(4), 1–10 (2018)
6. https://www.skyrme.com/kmthemes/web2.htm. Accessed 25 Apr 2020
7. Su, Y., Zheng, Z., Chen, J.: A multi-platform collaboration innovation ecosystem: the case of China. Manag. Decis. **56**(1), 125–142 (2018)
8. https://www.techopedia.com/definition/190/artificial-intelligence-ai. Accessed 17 Apr 2018
9. Worasinchai, L., Bechina, A.A.A.: The role of multinational corporations (MNC's) in developing R&D in Thailand: the knowledge flow between MNC's and university. Electron. J. Knowl. Manage. **8**(1), 171–180 (2010)
10. Zhao, F., Zeng, G.P.: Innovation ecosystem under multiple perspectives. Stud. Sci. Sci. **32** (12), 1781–1788 (2014)

A Note on Knowledge Management Education: Towards Implementing Active Learning Methods

Mieczysław L. Owoc[1]([⊠]) [iD] and Paweł Weichbroth[2] [iD]

[1] Wroclaw University of Economics and Business, Wroclaw, Poland
mieczyslaw.owoc@ue.wroc.pl
[2] Gdansk University of Technology, Gdansk, Poland
pawel.weichbroth@pg.edu.pl

Abstract. Knowledge Management as an area of education is still a big challenge for teachers and practitioners. Nevertheless, there are several useful teaching methods in active education, especially oriented towards courses where innovation and delivering dynamic knowledge are critical. The goal of the paper is to present and discuss criteria relevant in the selection of active educational methods supporting knowledge management courses. Examples of real cases from business schools seem to confirm the usefulness of a learner-centered approach.

Keywords: Knowledge · Management · Education · Active learning · Lectures

1 Introduction

Knowledge Management has become a crucial discipline in terms of the rational usage of different resources classified as knowledge granules [1–10]. Along this line of thinking, Babcock argues that "poor" knowledge-sharing practices cost the Fortune 500 companies $31.5 billion annually [11], while Greene acknowledges that 74% of organizations estimate that effective knowledge management practices increase company productivity by 10–40% [12]. From a business perspective, knowledge management (KM) is any system that facilitates the sharing, accessing, and updating of business knowledge for people in an organization. A report from 2015, elaborated by the Technology Service Industry Association (TSIA), shows that "KM is of growing interest to professional services, but so far formal processes are not well adopted" [13].

On the other hand, Coakes *et al.* claim that not enough attention has been paid to understanding the failures of knowledge management systems (KMS) [14]. One can observe that the rapid evolution of KMS solutions [15] has triggered the need to provide up-to-date learning resources, communicated in the most effective way. Although in many studies the problem of active teaching methods has been undertaken [16–26], only a few go so far as to investigate the extent of knowledge management [27–30]. Moreover, this study is motivated by the issues created by Poland's participation in the EU Erasmus+ programme [31], which aims to support education, training, youth and sport in Europe, with a budget of €14.7 billion over seven years (2014–2020).

© IFIP International Federation for Information Processing 2020
Published by Springer Nature Switzerland AG 2020
E. Mercier-Laurent (Ed.): AI4KM 2018, IFIP AICT 588, pp. 124–140, 2020.
https://doi.org/10.1007/978-3-030-52903-1_10

The objectives of this paper are to (1) examine the criteria possible to apply during the selection of active teaching methods, and (2) evaluate and rethink approaches in knowledge management education, based on three case studies. Note that the case study reported here was not conducted using any formal methodology, but was an attempt to have students actively learn different subjects and topics (e.g. Artificial Intelligence, Data Mining, Data Warehousing, Knowledge Management Systems) included in the Business Informatics curriculum at the Faculty of Management, Computer Science and Finance at Wroclaw University of Economics (WUE), as well as in the program of Data Science studies offered by Gdansk University of Technology (GUT).

The paper proceeds as follows. Section 2 presents the theoretical background of the research, and in Sects. 3 and 4, the core of Knowledge Management education is discussed. Active teaching methods are explained in Sect. 5 with a presentation of the methods implemented during participation in the DIMBI project. The final results of the study, with areas for future research, are itemized in the conclusion.

2 Theoretical Background

Studying both Business Informatics and Data Science requires motivated students. The motivation of students for a learning task is commonly defined in terms of the likeliness of achieving set goals [32]. In other words, if students have a considerable chance of success, their motivation will increase, and vice versa [33]. So in order to succeed, students need to obtain understanding, which requires involvement in learning. In view of this, the application of active teaching methods is a must, since engagement is not reflected by passive listeners in a classroom. To make the learning environment in KM-related courses more learner-centered, students need to be actively involved in learning activities.

In terms of critical and creative thinking, a meta-analysis by Cornelius-White, from 2007 [34], shows that learner-centered instruction (LCI) is associated with positive student outcomes: higher assessment scores, greater social connections and increased participation and initiation. Moreover, the analysis reports a reduction in disruptive and resistant behaviour, dropout rates, and school absences. On the other hand, some studies have reported that teacher-centered instruction (TCI) has been preferred because it provides clear expectations and specific learning goals [35–37]. Nevertheless, Granger et al. [38] compared LCI with TCI, and reported that the former approach facilitates higher learning outcomes, as well as having identified two mediators: student understanding and the self-efficacy of teachers.

The learner-centered paradigm focuses on the learners and their development rather than on the transmission of content [39]. In this regard, Smart et al. indicate that current learning theory suggests a different role for teachers – that of facilitators [40], advocating more active, inductive instruction in the classroom. Indeed, Stage et al. [41] emphasize the active construction of learners' own knowledge rather than passively receiving information transmitted to them from teachers and textbooks. In other words, knowledge should not be simply given to students, but they must construct their own meanings [42]. In this way, "teachers do less telling; students do more discovering" [43]. Therefore, the teacher's role is to design and lead the course in a way that facilitates a climate for effective learning by actively helping and encouraging students to learn from and with each other, consequently providing relevant feedback throughout the process [44].

3   Perspectives on Knowledge Management

To discuss the topic of teaching the subject of knowledge management, we begin by providing its definitions, introduced over the last 20 years. Having reviewed the literature, weare (unfortunately) still inclined to agree with Shin *et al.* [45] that "*a universally accepted definition of KM (knowledge management) does not exist yet*", which has also been confirmed by other researchers [46–49]. The definitions listed below, which are but a representative sample, are further briefly discussed.

Table 1. Perspectives on knowledge management.

Author (Year)	Perspective on knowledge management
De Jarnett (1996)	(…) is knowledge creation, which is followed by knowledge interpretation, knowledge dissemination and use, and knowledge retention and refinement [50]
Quintas *et al.* (1997)	(…) is the process of continually managing knowledge of all kinds to meet existing and emerging needs, to identify and exploit existing and acquired knowledge assets and to develop new opportunities [51]
Hibbard (1997)	(…) is the process of capturing a company's collective expertise wherever it resides - in databases, on paper, or in people's heads - and distributing it to wherever it can help produce the biggest payoff [52]
Bergeron (2003)	(…) is a deliberate, systematic business optimization strategy that selects, distills, stores, organizes, packages, and communicates information essential to the business of a company in a manner that improves employee performance and corporate competitiveness [53]
Jennex (2007)	(…) is the practice of selectively applying knowledge from previous experiences of decision making to current and future decision-making activities with the express purpose of improving the organization's effectiveness [54]
Handfield *et al.* (2015)	(…) organized and systematic process of generating and disseminating information, and selecting, distilling, and deploying explicit and tacit knowledge to create unique value that can be used to achieve a competitive advantage in the marketplace by an organization [55]

As follows from the above, the notion of knowledge management has been defined from different perspectives, and therefore in different ways. Firstly, a detailed reading of the definitions reveals that knowledge management is understood as relating to both theory and practice – for example, the definitions of De Jarnett [50] and Jennex [54], respectively. Secondly, Quintas *et al.* [51] and Hibbard [52], as well as Handfield *et al.* [55], began by using the word "process" which by dictionary definition means a series of actions that one takes in order to achieve a result [56]. Indeed, according to Alavi and Leider [57], knowledge management is largely regarded as a process involving various activities, and a minimum of four basic tasks must exist, namely creating, storing/retrieving, transferring and applying knowledge. Thirdly, individuals and learning are the priority facets of KM, since the vast majority of the existing literature covers these two related aspects, usually in an organizational context [58–65], and more recently focusing on the representation of empirical knowledge and methods and systems of reasoning [66–77].

Moreover, the wide range of definitions also reflects the fact that those authors studying the subject represent a broad spectrum of disciplines, such as computer science, engineering, management science, psychology, etc. Having said that, we conclude that knowledge management is a multidisciplinary field drawing from many subject areas. In addition, it is worth noting here that through diffusion with information technologies, knowledge management is still evolving and has become the fastest growing hub for creating innovations and shaping the future of business and science [78].

4   Knowledge Management Education

4.1   Education Providers

Chaudhry and Higgins (2003) report that knowledge management courses are mainly offered at the graduate level [79]. Their study covered five countries (Australia, Canada, Singapore, the UK and the USA), and in total embraced 37 km courses, the substance of which, in general, concerned topics such as business, computing and information, being part of the curricula in the departments and divisions of information systems.

In Poland, there are several universities in which knowledge management is present during the first (bachelor) and second (master of science) degrees of studies, offered by the most prestigious and the highest-ranking academic institutions, including:

- Adam Mickiewicz University in Poznan,
- AGH University of Science and Technology,
- Gdansk University of Technology,
- Jagiellonian University,
- Nicolaus Copernicus University,
- University of Wroclaw,
- Warsaw University of Technology,
- Wroclaw University of Economics and Business.

The course titles are generally the same, but in a few cases also concern intellectual capital or learning organizations.

4.2   Course Content

In total, the review encompasses the content of 10 course syllabuses, offered by particular departments. Their later synthesis indicates that the following topics are frequently included (Table 2).

Table 2. Curriculum areas and topics in knowledge management courses.

Area	Topics
1. Foundations	• definitions and concepts related to the theory of data, information, knowledge, wisdom and vision; • knowledge management theory; • forms of knowledge (tacit, explicit); • sources of knowledge: individual, groups, communities, crowdsourcing, and know-hows, instructions and ontologies; • knowledge workers and intellectual capital; • knowledge-based organizations
2. Technology	• the evolution of IT systems (expert systems, knowledge-based systems, business intelligence systems); • intranets, extranets, collaboration and social network tools, • corporate portals; • requirements elicitation and analysis; • data, information and knowledge architectures and architects; • examples of IT tools and systems
3. Process	• knowledge management models; • knowledge acquisition and mapping; • organization and categorization of knowledge resources; • developing and maintaining knowledge repositories; • auditing and tracking knowledge repositories
4. Applications	• lessons learned, case studies and success stories of IT tools and systems design, implementations and deployments; • considerations for knowledge management applications in different domains, sectors (public, private) and industries; • student hands-on activity: designing, implementing and deploying KM services in an organization
5. Strategies	• categories of knowledge management strategies; • the process of knowledge management strategy development; • sustainable development of an organization's intellectual capital; • human resources department and its support and responsibilities in employee development;

First of all, we grouped frequently included topics into five categories. It seems that these areas can be considered as the foundations of knowledge management lectures. Secondly, course content in general emphasizes the role of the individual, even though the labels strongly indicate the organizational context. Thirdly, in a few courses, law-oriented topics were included in the end; however, we concur that these are not the core substance of the KM domain. Fourthly, a pro-sharing culture and practices were also listed as essential indicators in building knowledge-based organizations. Finally, the specified classification of KM topics is nonetheless an open list that can be supplemented as desired. In view of this, for the purpose of classification into a consistent arrangement, we have rephrased the topics and rearranged them under the principles of qualitative synthesis research (keeping the substance of the content intact).

4.3   Identified Differences

The bulk of course syllabuses varied strongly in general. While some are focused on developing students' soft skills, others are strongly oriented towards a particular IT platform with the aim of learning how to design and implement specific tasks. In particular, the latter aim to demonstrate how to capture and share key information within an organization to enable effective decision-making, as well as how to implement a communication strategy where teams can switch to efficient searching, sorting and sharing of knowledge assets. Whereas the former type puts an emphasis on actively engaging students in reflective exercises, systematically conducted throughout the course. In so doing, such courses therefore have specific learning outcomes that firmly correspond to contemporary knowledge management theory.

5   Active Teaching Approach

5.1   The Learning Pyramid

A crucial category in the education process is the approach to learning. The approach can be identified with ideas or a set of principles about the nature of learning. Current analyses of the effectiveness of particular approaches in education prove that traditional forms of delivering knowledge through lecturing are not successful. This problem is frequently presented in the Learning Pyramid, embracing the basic orientation in teaching nowadays (see Fig. 1 below).

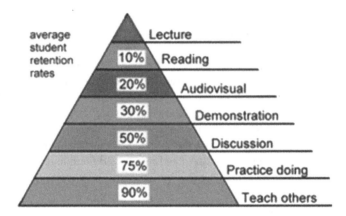

Fig. 1. The learning pyramid [80].

The picture reflecting the average student retention rates (as a simplified measure of delivered knowledge) proves the superiority of more active approaches (in this Figure, referenced by the three layers placed at the lowest parts of the pyramid: discussion, practice doing and teach others) irrespective of educational areas. There is a vast amount of teaching methods or techniques which represent approaches covering several layers of the learning pyramid [81–83]. Some of them are oriented towards teachers while others towards learners. Learner-oriented education can be identified mostly with active teaching methods.

5.2   Active Teaching Methods

There is a need for a diversification into two essential categories in the demonstration of particular approaches: teaching methods and teaching techniques. A method can be defined as a description of the way that knowledge is delivered to learners during the instructional process or during the training activities of learners (for example: making projects). One may also add that a method is a systematic way of doing something according to an earlier established approach. A teaching technique can be identified with a guideline for any teaching activity (for example: mind mapping). Therefore, teaching techniques are more oriented towards the implementation of specific ways of delivering knowledge to or shaping the capabilities of learners. To sum up, a learning approach determines the teaching methods and, in turn, particular methods require the adequate teaching technique(s). We focus in the paper on teaching methods which are typical for active approaches in education, assuming the implementation of relevant teaching techniques in such a context.

There are several taxonomies of teaching methods which stress the critical features of a particular typology of methods [84–86]. We have reduced the list of available teaching methods to the following items:

- **Collaborative Virtual Classrooms** – interpreted as an online learning environment that allows live interaction between the tutor and the learners as they are participating in learning activities. Collaboration among participants in the established learning environment are crucial in this method [87–89].

- **Brainstorming** – identified with the creativeness of participants in solving problems by gathering a list of solutions in a spontaneous way. Independent and unlimited proposals of ideas for finding conclusions by members of a team, respectful of one another, are specific in this method [90–92].
- **Making Projects** – oriented towards the practical implementation of theoretical domain knowledge and trained abilities to create a new solution in the defined environment. The project method, performed through several steps, allows students to deal with potential circumstances playing more and more the role of managers; individual or team endeavours in obtaining the defined goals are typical in this method [93–95].
- **Role Playing** – an approach of learning focused on exploring using students' realistic situations by interacting with other people in order to develop experiences and trial different strategies in a supported environment. This method allows for progress in understanding and improving different positions of team members [96–98].
- **The 'Flipped Classroom'** – an instructional blended learning strategy related to delivering instructional content outside of the classroom through forcing students to elaborate teaching materials themselves. It denotes a more individual method of teaching, oriented towards the investigation of knowledge acquisition [99–101].
- **Case Studies** – an instructional method referring to assigned scenarios based on situations in which students observe, analyse, register, implement and summarize, or recommend. The main advantage of this method is dealing with real problems and ways of creating solutions [102–104].
- **Discussions** – a group activity involving a teacher as well as students to define a problem and search for its solutions; therefore, this constructive process involves listening, thinking and, as a result, exchanging ideas. Again, the activeness of team members and improving ways of argumentation are specific in this method [105–107].
- **Game-based Learning** – a teaching method consisting of the exploration of different components of games. Playing a game motivates participants and shapes capabilities in obtaining the defined aims. Social aspects and respecting rules are important in this method [108–110].

In all the presented teaching methods students are encouraged to be active and, in most cases, they should work as co-operators or competitors. Regardless of the implemented teaching methods, improvements in the capabilities of students in the knowledge management domain are related with the following objectives:

- **capture knowledge**: this goal can be achieved by creating knowledge management repositories. Those will consist of structured documents with knowledge embedded in them, such as memos, reports, presentations and articles, which are stored in a way that they may be easily retrieved;
- **improve knowledge**: access with the aim of facilitating the processes of knowledge transfer between individuals and between organizations;

- **enhance the knowledge environment**: by proactively facilitating and rewarding knowledge creation, transfer and use;
- **facilitate knowledge management**: as an asset, some companies are including their intellectual capital in the balance sheet, others are leveraging their knowledge assets to generate new income from or to reduce costs with their patent base.

Arguably, the purpose of education is to open the minds of students and equip them with the wherewithal – essentially knowledge – with which to envisage and create the preferred future (and not merely respond to circumstances or events). In the age of globalization, accelerating technological change and increased competition, knowledge management can help educational institutions - be they public, private or the object of public-private partnerships - improve teaching for better learning outcomes. In education, as elsewhere, knowledge management can bring together people, processes and technologies to enable the discussed institutions to accomplish their missions. The objectives of KM studies still remain as follows (in terms of educational approaches):

- diversification of learning levels;
- different aims of teaching;
- variety of the components of education.

The list of teaching methods previously presented can be implemented in knowledge management teaching. Undoubtedly, particular teaching methods fulfil the assumed objectives of knowledge management education. However, one more thing must be discussed in the context of successful teaching, namely organizational learning, in which individual as well as team aspects should be included. The general idea of this perspective is presented below (Fig. 2).

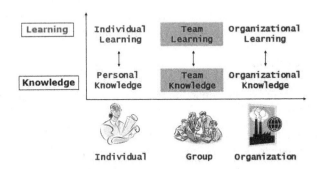

Fig. 2. Organizational learning and knowledge management perspective [111].

Any of the discussed active teaching methods can be useful in supporting the acquisition of individual and team (and finally organizational) knowledge and the training capabilities of the participants. However, the question arises of how to select the most adequate method for particular educational institutions.

5.3   Selection Criteria for Active Teaching Methods

The general idea of the selection of teaching methods is presented in the Figure below. The rationale behind the choice of the relevant method should incorporate the participants of the educational processes, the subjects to be taught and the learning infrastructure. The interrelationships between the discovered factors of the selection can be a base for the proposed steps in the general choice concept scenario (Fig. 3).

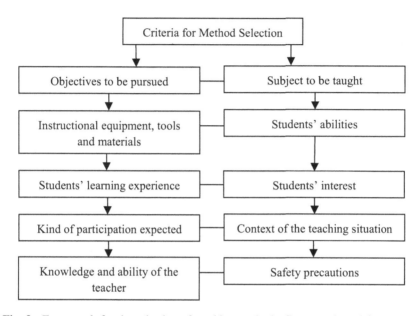

Fig. 3. Framework for the selection of teaching methods. Source: adopted from [112].

The criteria embrace teacher properties (knowledge and ability), student characteristics (abilities, experience and interests) and other determinants: equipment, tools, and the teaching context.

The described approach for the selection of teaching methods has been applied in the DIMBI (Developing the Innovative Methodology of Teaching Business Informatics) framework project. The main goals of the project embrace:

- **analysis** of existing teaching methods applied in Business Informatics education,
- **preparation** of teaching methods useful in BI courses,
- **elaboration** of e-learning platforms supporting BI teaching,
- **sharing** of Active Books useful in performing selected BI courses.

The results of this project are available for students studying Business Informatics at the Bachelor level. Initially, the results were implemented in three partner universities: Wroclaw University of Economics (WUE), Varna University of Economics (VUE) and Jan Wyzykowski University (JWU) in Polkowice. The initial results of the implemented active teaching methods are presented in Table 1. The research was limited to education in Knowledge Management using a questionnaire addressed to teaching staff.

In particular, the following objectives were investigated in the research:

- understanding the objectives of Knowledge Management in the Business Informatics field of study,
- understanding the process of knowledge acquisition from data in the context of KM,
- gathering the skills necessary to collect project stakeholders' requirements in terms of the KM domain as an element of BI education,
- discovering the most important features and capabilities of BI tools supporting Knowledge Management (Table 3).

Table 3. Implemented teaching methods in KM education

Active teaching method	WUE	VUE	JWU
Collaborative virtual classroom	1	1	2
Brainstorming	2	3	2
Making projects	3	2	3
Role playing	1	1	2
The flipped classroom	1	0	1
Case studies	3	2	3
Discussions	2	2	3
Game-based learning	1	0	1

0 – not implemented, 1 – initial stage, 2 – partly implemented, 3 – fully implemented.

The initial results of the research confirm the usability of the selected active teaching methods in KM education. The methods most often used were Making Projects and Case Studies. In the case of KM education, students entered companies and solved problems (mostly working in teams) defined by company managers. On the other hand, academic staff very rarely used Flipped Classroom and Game-based Learning. The reason was the lack of tradition in implementing these methods (Flipped Classroom) as well as the lack of attractive tools (Game-based Learning).

6   Conclusions and Future Research

In an atmosphere of increased external and internal pressures for improvements in education, the need for effective teaching methods has never been greater – yet there is a real risk of competency gaps. However, the real need for improvements in Knowledge Management education seems to be obvious. Active teaching methods should be implemented in Knowledge Management courses on a wider scale. The implementation of active teaching methods in Knowledge Management has been proposed in ongoing educational projects.

Despite the challenges to implement learner-centered instruction (LCI) by many individuals and organizations – typical for active teaching methods – LCI has not been included in the "Development strategy of higher education in Poland until 2020" [113], prepared by Ernst & Young and Gdansk Institute for Market Economics. We believe that the six strategic goals, namely diversity, openness, mobility, competition, effectiveness and transparency, should be reconsidered in terms of the learner-centered paradigm and active teaching methods in the next agenda.

Our future research will cover the following topics: applying a hybrid way of teaching (different scenarios for KM topics), the utilization of ICT tools to monitor the results of the inception of active teaching methods, and eventually developing and assimilating these methods to teaching areas through existing and new courses in Business Informatics studies.

References

1. Owoc, M.L.: From local to global validation of a knowledge base. Prace Naukowe Akademii Ekonomicznej we Wrocławiu (772), 100–109 (1997)
2. Owoc, M.L.: Measuring aspects of knowledge validation. Prace Naukowe Akademii Ekonomicznej we Wrocławiu (787), 170–181 (1998)
3. Jakubczyc, J.A., Owoc, M.L.: Knowledge management and artificial intelligence. Argumenta Oeconomica 1(6) (1998)
4. Mercier-Laurent, E., Jakubczyc, J., Owoc, M.L.: What is knowledge management? Prace Naukowe Akademii Ekonomicznej we Wrocławiu (815), 9–21 (1999)
5. Owoc, M.L., Ochmańska, M.: Towards knowledge validation theory. Prace Naukowe Akademii Ekonomicznej we Wrocławiu (815), 49–60 (1999)
6. Owoc, M.L., Ochmanska, M., Gladysz, T.: On principles of knowledge validation. In: Vermesan, A., Coenen, F. (eds.) Validation and Verification of Knowledge Based Systems, pp. 25–35. Springer, Boston (1999). https://doi.org/10.1007/978-1-4757-6916-6_2
7. Bonner, R., Galant, V., Owoc, M.: Features of decision trees as a technique of knowledge modelling. In: 1999 The Workshop on Computer Science and Information Technologies (CSIT), pp. 135–137 (1999)
8. Owoc, M.L., Galant, V.: Validation of rule-based systems generated by classification algorithms. In: Zupančič, J., Wojtkowski, W., Wojtkowski, W.G., Wrycza, S. (eds.) Evolution and Challenges in System Development, pp. 459–467. Springer, Boston (1999). https://doi.org/10.1007/978-1-4615-4851-5_42
9. Jakubczyc, J.A., Matouk, K., Owoc, M.L.: Applications of intelligent systems in Poland-our present state of observing. Prace Naukowe Akademii Ekonomicznej we Wrocławiu, Pozyskiwanie wiedzy i zarządzanie wiedzą, 168–177 (2003)
10. Owoc, M.L.: Knowledgebases: a management context and development determinants. In: Proceedings of 2003 Informing Science and Information Technology Education Conference, Pori, pp. 1193–1199 (2003)
11. Babcock, P.: Shedding Light on Knowledge Management. HR Magazine (2004). https://www.shrm.org/hr-today/news/hr-magazine/Pages/0504covstory.aspx. Accessed 21 Dec 2019
12. Greene, J.: What Is Knowledge Management, and Why Is It Important? (2006). https://www.askspoke.com/blog/knowledge-management/knowledge-management-importance/. Accessed 21 Dec 2019
13. Technology Service Industry Association: What is Currently shaping knowledge sharing? Report (2015). www.tsia.com. Accessed 21 Dec 2019

14. Coakes, E., Amar, A.D., Granados, M.L.: Success or failure in knowledge management systems: a universal issue. In: Dwivedi, Y.K., Henriksen, H.Z., Wastell, D., De', R. (eds.) TDIT 2013. IAICT, vol. 402, pp. 39–56. Springer, Heidelberg (2013). https://doi.org/10. 1007/978-3-642-38862-0_3
15. Alavi, M., Leidner, D.: Knowledge management systems: issues, challenges, and benefits. Commun. Assoc. Inf. Syst. 1(1), 7 (1999)
16. Benzing, C., Christ, P.: A survey of teaching methods among economics faculty. J. Econ. Educ. 28(2), 182–188 (1997)
17. Bonner, S.E.: Choosing teaching methods based on learning objectives: an integrative framework. Issues Account. Educ. 14(1), 11–15 (1999)
18. Haidet, P., Morgan, R.O., O'malley, K., Moran, B.J., Richards, B.F.: A controlled trial of active versus passive learning strategies in a large group setting. Adv. Health Sci. Educ. 9 (1), 15–27 (2004). https://doi.org/10.1023/B:AHSE.0000012213.62043.45
19. Bankauskienė, N., Augustinienė, A., Čiučiulkienė, N.: The expression of teacher competencies in action research field: the case-based study of KTU teacher education program pedagogy. In: European Conference on Educational Research, pp. 7–10. University College Dublin (2005)
20. Calinon, S., Billard, A.: Active teaching in robot programming by demonstration. In: RO-MAN 2007-The 16th IEEE International Symposium on Robot and Human Interactive Communication, pp. 702–707. IEEE (2007)
21. Abebe, T.T., Davidson, L.M., Biru, F.: The role of instructors in implementing communicative language teaching methodology. Res. Humanit. Soc. Sci. 2(3), 52–62 (2012)
22. Močinić, S.N.: Active teaching strategies in higher education. Metodički obzori: časopis za odgojno-obrazovnu teoriju i praksu 7(15), 97–105 (2012)
23. Jarahi, L.: Evaluation of teaching through lecture with new methods of student-centered teaching in medical students. Future Med. Educ. J. 3(4), 6–9 (2013)
24. Barbera-Ribera, T., Estelles-Miguel, S., Dema-Perez, C.M.: Student opinion on the application of active methodologies. In: Peris-Ortiz, M., Merigó Lindahl, J.M. (eds.) Sustainable Learning in Higher Education. ITKM, pp. 157–167. Springer, Cham (2015). https://doi.org/10.1007/978-3-319-10804-9_12
25. Jeronen, E., Palmberg, I., Yli-Panula, E.: Teaching methods in biology education and sustainability education including outdoor education for promoting sustainability—a literature review. Educ. Sci. 7(1), 1 (2017)
26. Andres, H.P.: Active teaching to manage course difficulty and learning motivation. J. Furth. High. Educ. 43(2), 220–235 (2019)
27. Bontis, N., Girardi, J.: Teaching knowledge management and intellectual capital lessons: an empirical examination of the TANGO simulation. Int. J. Technol. Manag. 20(5–8), 545–555 (2000)
28. Tippins, M.J.: Implementing knowledge management in academia: teaching the teachers. Int. J. Educ. Manag. 17(7), 339–345 (2003)
29. Chua, A.Y.: The design and implementation of a simulation game for teaching knowledge management. J. Am. Soc. Inf. Sci. Technol. 56(11), 1207–1216 (2005)
30. Ghafarian Shirazi, H.R., Qhorbani, M., Afrasyabi, R.: A study on the role and importance of information technology in the establishment of knowledge management in training and education. Eur. Online J. Nat. Soc. Sci. 2(3) (2014)
31. Erasmus+. https://erasmusplus.org.pl/. Accessed 21 Dec 2019
32. Moura, I.C., van Hattum-Janssen, N.: Teaching a CS introductory course: an active approach. Comput. Educ. 56(2), 475–483 (2011)
33. Schunk, D.H.: Learning Theories an Educational Perspective, 6th edn. Pearson, Boston (2012)

34. Cornelius-White, J.: Learner-centered teacher-student relationships are effective: a meta-analysis. Rev. Educ. Res. **77**(1), 113–143 (2007)
35. Vatterott, C.: Student-focused instruction: balancing limits with freedom in the middle grades. Middle Sch. J. **27**(2), 28–38 (1995)
36. Wiggins, J.: Teaching for Musical Understanding. McGraw-Hill Humanities Social, Boston (2001)
37. Verkuyten, M.: Making teachers accountable for students' disruptive classroom behaviour. Br. J. Sociol. Educ. **23**(1), 107–122 (2002)
38. Granger, E.M., Bevis, T.H., Saka, Y., Southerland, S.A., Sampson, V., Tate, R.L.: The efficacy of student-centered instruction in supporting science learning. Science **338**(6103), 105–108 (2012)
39. IGI Global Dictionary. What is Learner-Centered Teaching. https://www.igi-global.com/dictionary/creating-collaboration-in-global-online-learning/40896
40. Smart, K.L., Witt, C., Scott, J.P.: Toward learner-centered teaching: An inductive approach. Bus. Commun. Q. **75**(4), 392–403 (2012)
41. Stage, F.K., Muller, P.A., Kinzie, J., Simmons, A.: Creating learner centered class-rooms: what does learning theory have to say? ERIC Clearinghouse on Higher Education and the Association for the Study of Higher Education, Washington, DC (1998)
42. Uden, L., Liu, K., Shank, G.: Linking radical constructivism and semiotics to design a constructivist learning environment. J. Comput. High. Educ. **12**(2), 34–51 (2001). https://doi.org/10.1007/BF02940955
43. Weimer, M.: Learner-Centered Teaching: Five Key Changes to Practice. Jossey-Bass, San Francisco (2002)
44. Cheang, K.I.: Effect of learner-centered teaching on motivation and learning strategies in a third-year pharmacotherapy course. Am. J. Pharm. Educ. **73**(3), 42 (2009)
45. Shin, M., Holden, T., Schmidt, R.A.: From knowledge theory to management practice: towards an integrated approach. Inf. Process. Manag. **37**(2), 335–355 (2001)
46. Schlegelmilch, B.B., Penz, E.: Knowledge management in marketing. Mark. Rev. **3**(1), 5–19 (2002)
47. Adler, N., Shani, R.: In search of an alternative framework for the creation of actionable knowledge: table-tennis research at Ericsson. In: Research in Organizational Change and Development, pp. 43–79. Emerald Group Publishing Limited (2001)
48. Sharma, R.K.: Understanding organizational learning through knowledge management. J. Inf. Knowl. Manag. **2**(04), 343–352 (2003)
49. Sokół, A., Figurska, I.: Creativity as one of the core competencies of studying knowledge workers (2017)
50. De Jarnett, L.: Knowledge the latest thing. Inf. Strategy Exec. J. **12**(pt 2), 3–5 (1996)
51. Quintas, P., Lefrere, P., Jones, G.: Knowledge management: a strategic agenda. Long Range Plan. **30**(3), 385–391 (1997)
52. Hibbard, J.: Knowing what we know. InformationWeek **653**, 46–54 (1997)
53. Bergeron, B.: Essentials of Knowledge Management, vol. 28. Wiley, Hoboken (2003)
54. Jennex, M.E.: What is knowledge management? In: Knowledge Management in Modern Organizations, pp. 1–9. IGI Global (2007)
55. Handfield, R.B., Cousins, P.D., Lawson, B., Petersen, K.J.: How can supply management really improve performance? A knowledge-based model of alignment capabilities. J. Supply Chain Manag. **51**(3), 3–17 (2015)
56. Cambridge Dictionary. https://dictionary.cambridge.org/dictionary/english/process. Accessed 23 Dec 2019
57. Alavi, M., Leidner, D.E.: Knowledge management and knowledge management systems: conceptual foundations and research issues. MIS Q., 107–136 (2001)

58. Leja, K.: Organizational creation of knowledge in universities (2007)
59. Owoc, M., Marciniak, K.: Knowledge management as foundation of smart university. In: 2013 Federated Conference on Computer Science and Information Systems, pp. 1267–1272. IEEE (2013)
60. Kutzner, I., Hauke, K., Marciniak, K., Owoc, M.: Creation of the urban knowledge portal: e-learning and knowledge inventor context. In: 2015 11th International Conference on Semantics, Knowledge and Grids (SKG), pp. 97–104. IEEE (2015)
61. Koohang, A., Paliszkiewicz, J., Gołuchowski, J.: Trust, knowledge management, and organizational performance: predictors of success in leadership. Intuit. Trust Anal. **117**(3), 83–105 (2017)
62. Owoc, M., Weichbroth, P., Żuralski, K.: Towards better understanding of context-aware knowledge transformation. In: 2017 Federated Conference on Computer Science and Information Systems (FedCSIS), pp. 1123–1126. IEEE (2017)
63. Owoc, M., Hołowińska, K.: Differentiation of supporting methods of business informatics teaching offered by selected educational portals. Informatyka Ekonomiczna **2**(48), 54–66 (2018)
64. Basińska, B., Leja, K., Szuflita-Żurawska, M.: Positive Management of Universities: A Model of Motivation to Strive for Scientific Excellence (2019)
65. Owoc, M., Weichbroth, P.: Dynamical aspects of knowledge evolution. In: Mercier-Laurent, E., Boulanger, D. (eds.) AI4KM 2017. IAICT, vol. 571, pp. 52–65. Springer, Cham (2019). https://doi.org/10.1007/978-3-030-29904-0_5
66. Kwiatkowska, M., Kielan, K., Michalik, K.: A fuzzy-semiotic framework for modeling imprecision in the assessment of depression. In: IFSA/EUSFLAT Conference, pp. 1717–1722 (2009)
67. von Michalik, K., Kwiatkowska, M., Kielan, K.: Application of knowledge-engineering methods in medical knowledge management. In: Seising, R., Tabacchi, M. (eds.) Fuzziness and Medicine: Philosophical Reflections and Application Systems in Health Care. Studies in Fuzziness and Soft Computing, vol. 302, pp. 205–214. Springer, Heidelberg (2013). https://doi.org/10.1007/978-3-642-36527-0_14
68. Owoc, M.L., Ahmed, A.S.: Data warehouse as a source of knowledge acquisition. An empirical study. In: 2014 Federated Conference on Computer Science and Information Systems, pp. 1421–1430. IEEE (2014)
69. Goczyła, K., Waloszek, A., Waloszek, W.: Contextualizing a knowledge base by approximation - a case study. In: Kozielski, S., Mrozek, D., Kasprowski, P., Małysiak-Mrozek, B., Kostrzewa, D. (eds.) BDAS 2014. CCIS, vol. 424, pp. 112–123. Springer, Cham (2014). https://doi.org/10.1007/978-3-319-06932-6_12
70. Owoc, M., Weichbroth, P.: Validation model for discovered web user navigation patterns. In: Mercier-Laurent, E., Boulanger, D. (eds.) AI4KM 2012. IAICT, vol. 422, pp. 38–52. Springer, Heidelberg (2014). https://doi.org/10.1007/978-3-642-54897-0_3
71. Owoc, M.L.: Benefits of knowledge acquisition systems for management. An empirical study. In: 2015 Federated Conference on Computer Science and Information Systems (FedCSIS), pp. 1691–1698. IEEE (2015)
72. Ossowska, K., Szewc, L., Weichbroth, P., Garnik, I., Sikorski, M.: Exploring an ontological approach for user requirements elicitation in the design of online virtual agents. In: Wrycza, S. (ed.) SIGSAND/PLAIS 2016. LNBIP, vol. 264, pp. 40–55. Springer, Cham (2016). https://doi.org/10.1007/978-3-319-46642-2_3
73. Owoc, M., Hauke, K., Weichbroth, P.: Knowledge-grid modelling for academic purposes. In: Mercier-Laurent, E., Boulanger, D. (eds.) AI4KM 2015. IAICT, vol. 497, pp. 1–14. Springer, Cham (2016). https://doi.org/10.1007/978-3-319-55970-4_1

74. Kuciapski, M.: A model of mobile technologies acceptance for knowledge transfer by employees. J. Knowl. Manag. **21**(5), 1053–1076 (2017)
75. Kaplanski, P., Weichbroth, P.: Cognitum ontorion: knowledge representation and reasoning system. In: Pełech-Pilichowski, T., Mach-Król, M., Olszak, C.M. (eds.) Advances in Business ICT: New Ideas from Ongoing Research. SCI, vol. 658, pp. 27–43. Springer, Cham (2017). https://doi.org/10.1007/978-3-319-47208-9_3
76. Owoc, M., Hauke, K., Marciniak, K.: Dynamic ontology supporting local government. In: Mercier-Laurent, E., Boulanger, D. (eds.) AI4KM 2016. IAICT, vol. 518, pp. 36–49. Springer, Cham (2018). https://doi.org/10.1007/978-3-319-92928-6_3
77. Weichbroth, P.: Fluent editor and controlled natural language in ontology development. Int. J. Artif. Intell. Tools **28**(04), 1940007 (2019)
78. Nowacki, R., Bachnik, K.: Innovations within knowledge management. J. Bus. Res. **69**(5), 1577–1581 (2016)
79. Chaudhry, A.S., Higgins, S.: On the need for a multidisciplinary approach to education for knowledge management. Libr. Rev. (2003)
80. Training Laboratories, Bethel (Maine)
81. Jacobsen, D.A., Eggen, P.D., Kauchak, D.P.: Methods for Teaching: Promoting Student Learning. Prentice Hall, Upper Saddle River (2002)
82. Bass, B.: Action research study of classical teaching methods vs. active learning methods in the middle school social studies classroom. Culminating Experience Action Research Projects, vol. 18, Part 2, 26 (2016)
83. Christie, M., de Graaff, E.: The philosophical and pedagogical underpinnings of active learning in engineering education. Eur. J. Eng. Educ. **42**(1), 5–16 (2017)
84. Silberman, M.: Active Learning: 101 Strategies To Teach Any Subject. Prentice-Hall, Des Moines (1996)
85. Armbruster, P., Patel, M., Johnson, E., Weiss, M.: Active learning and student-centered pedagogy improve student attitudes and performance in introductory biology. CBE–Life Sci. Educ. **8**(3), 203–213 (2009)
86. Konopka, C.L., Adaime, M.B., Mosele, P.H.: Active teaching and learning methodologies: some considerations. Creat. Educ. **6**(14), 1536 (2015)
87. Bouras, C., Giannaka, E., Tsiatsos, T.: Virtual collaboration spaces: the EVE community. In: Proceedings of the 2003 Symposium on Applications and the Internet, pp. 48–55. IEEE (2003)
88. Di Blas, N., Poggi, C.: European virtual classrooms: building effective "virtual" educational experiences. Virtual Reality **11**(2–3), 129–143 (2007). https://doi.org/10.1007/s10055-006-0060-4
89. Bower, M., Lee, M.J., Dalgarno, B.: Collaborative learning across physical and virtual worlds: Factors supporting and constraining learners in a blended reality environment. Br. J. Edu. Technol. **48**(2), 407–430 (2017)
90. Sharafi-Nejad, M., Raftari, S., Ismail, S.A.M.M., Eng, L.S.: Prior knowledge activation through brainstorming to enhance Malaysian EFL learners' reading comprehension. Int. J. Linguist. **8**(2), 187–198 (2016)
91. Unin, N., Bearing, P.: Brainstorming as a way to approach student-centered learning in the ESL classroom. Procedia-Soc. Behav. Sci. **224**, 605–612 (2016)
92. Weichbroth, P.: Facing the brainstorming theory. A case of requirements elicitation. Studia Ekonomiczne **296**, 151–162 (2016)
93. Livingstone, D., Lynch, K.: Group project work and student-centred active learning: Two different experiences. Stud. High. Educ. **25**(3), 325–345 (2000)
94. Graham, R., Crawley, E.: Making projects work: a review of transferable best practice approaches to engineering project-based learning in the UK. Eng. Educ. **5**(2), 41–49 (2010)

95. Chandrasekaran, S., Stojcevski, A., Littlefair, G.A., Joordens, M.: Learning through projects in engineering education. In: SEFI 2012: Engineering Education 2020: Meet the Future: Proceedings of the 40th SEFI Annual Conference 2012. European Society for Engineering Education (SEFI) (2012)

96. McLaughlan, R.G., Kirkpatrick, D.: Online roleplay: design for active learning. Eur. J. Eng. Educ. **29**(4), 477–490 (2004)

97. Joyner, B., Young, L.: Teaching medical students using role play: twelve tips for successful role plays. Med. Teach. **28**(3), 225–229 (2006)

98. Poling, D.A., Hupp, J.M.: Active learning through role playing: virtual babies in a child development course. Coll. Teach. **57**(4), 221–228 (2009)

99. Stone, B.B.: Flip your classroom to increase active learning and student engagement. In: Proceedings from 28th Annual Conference on Distance Teaching & Learning, Madison, Wisconsin, USA (2012)

100. Desai, P., Vijayalakshmi, M.: Flipped classroom: an efficient pedagogical tool to teach a course for final year computer science and engineering graduate students. J. Eng. Educ. Transform., 306–310 (2015)

101. Boevé, A.J., Meijer, R.R., Bosker, R.J., Vugteveen, J., Hoekstra, R., Albers, C.J.: Implementing the flipped classroom: an exploration of study behaviour and student performance. High. Educ. **74**(6), 1015–1032 (2017). https://doi.org/10.1007/s10734-016-0104-y

102. Holley, E.A.: Engaging engineering students in geoscience through case studies and active learning. J. Geosci. Educ. **65**(3), 240–249 (2017)

103. Carloye, L.: Mini-case studies: Small infusions of active learning for large-lecture courses. J. Coll. Sci. Teach. **46**(6), 63 (2017)

104. Nkhoma, M., Sriratanaviriyakul, N., Quang, H.L.: Using case method to enrich students' learning outcomes. Act. Learn. High Educ. **18**(1), 37–50 (2017)

105. Campbell, C., Blair, H.: Learning the active way: creating interactive lectures to promote student learning. In: Handbook of Research on Pedagogical Models for Next-Generation Teaching and Learning, pp. 21-37. IGI Global (2018)

106. Yamada, A., Yamada, R.: The new movement of active learning in Japanese higher education: the analysis of active learning case in Japanese graduate programs. In: Active Learning. IntechOpen (2018)

107. Wood, A.K., Galloway, R.K., Sinclair, C., Hardy, J.: Teacher-student discourse in active learning lectures: case studies from undergraduate physics. Teach. High. Educ. **23**(7), 818–834 (2018)

108. Przybylek, A., Olszewski, M.K.: Adopting collaborative games into Open Kanban. In: 2016 Federated Conference on Computer Science and Information Systems (FedCSIS), pp. 1539–1543. IEEE (2016)

109. Yukselturk, E., Altıok, S., Başer, Z.: Using game-based learning with kinect technology in foreign language education course. J. Educ. Technol. Soc. **21**(3), 159–173 (2018)

110. Przybyłek, A., Kotecka, D.: Making agile retrospectives more awesome. In: 2017 Federated Conference on Computer Science and Information Systems, pp. 1211–1216. IEEE (2017)

111. Wikimedia Commons. Organizational Learning and KM (2018). https://commons.wikimedia.org/wiki/File:Organizational_Learning_and_KM.jpg. Accessed 18 Jan 2020

112. Madrid, M.: Teaching Methods (2013). https://www.slideshare.net/MariaMarthaManette Madrid/teaching-methods-21761134. Accessed 19 Jan 2020

113. Strategia rozwoju szkolnictwa wyższego w Polsce do 2020 roku. http://cpp.amu.edu.pl/pdf/SSW2020_strategia.pdf. Accessed 19 Jan 2020

Intellect Modeling Kit

Konstantin M. Golubev[(⊠)]

General Knowledge Machine Research Group, Kiev, Ukraine
gkm-ekp@users.sf.net
http://gkm-ekp.sf.net

Abstract. It is presentation of technology called Intellect Modeling developed with idea of amplification of human intellect and as an alternative to traditional Artificial Intelligence. The goal is to assist human intellect on every step of its activity, accept human knowledge and develop new knowledge together with people. The activity of Intellect Modeling applications could be verified by human expert on every stage. Intellect Modeling Kit is an open-source project located at Sourceforge repository http://sourceforge.net/projects/gkm-ekp.

Keywords: Intellect Modeling · Artificial Intelligence · Adaptive learning · Just-in-time knowledge · General Knowledge Machine · Electronic Knowledge Publishing

1 Introduction

Intellect Modeling Kit (IMK) is a system for assisting intellectual activity during the following steps:

1. **Observation - getting data and information**
   The component gkmforms.exe creates specialized site accessible with Web browser for interaction with user
2. **Producing propositions, based on the knowledge**
   The component gkm2017b.exe produces propositions based on user input and internal e-knowledge
3. **Selection and verification of the most appropriate propositions**
   The specialized site for interaction with user created by component gkmforms.exe produces ranged propositions list with detailed explanations
4. **Memorizing - converting data to information and new knowledge item creation**
   The component soz2017b.exe creates e-knowledge database containing human knowledge that could be used on step 1
5. **Abstraction finding – building artificial objects representing group of real objects, featuring typical signs of group**
   The component abs2017b.exe performs tasks as **Data Mining, Big Data and Natural Cluster Analysis** to find groups of similar objects and regularities they are based on.

© IFIP International Federation for Information Processing 2020
Published by Springer Nature Switzerland AG 2020
E. Mercier-Laurent (Ed.): AI4KM 2018, IFIP AICT 588, pp. 141–155, 2020.
https://doi.org/10.1007/978-3-030-52903-1_11

2   IMK Components and Interaction

2.1   IMK Components

IMK includes the following objects:

- `v2017b.zip` – sources of components soz2017b.f, gkm2017b.f, abs2017b.f, gkmforms.bas, gkminter.php, settings, ini and dat files, binaries for Windows and Linux, pictures and icons.
- `renais.zip` – sources for **ELECTRONIC KNOWLEDGE SYSTEM ON RENAISSANCE PAINTING**
- `gestures.zip` – sources for **ELECTRONIC KNOWLEDGE SYSTEM ON LANGUAGE OF GESTURES**
- `avitamin.zip` – sources for **ELECTRONIC KNOWLEDGE SYSTEM ON AVITAMINOSIS**
- `gfortran4.zip` – portable compiler of GNU Fortran v4.7 for Windows with **IMK** sources in bin directory
- `freebas.zip` – portable compiler of Free Basic v1.04 for Windows with IMK sources
- `geany.zip` – portable IDE for Windows for Fortran, Basic and PHP
- `kmeleon.zip` – portable browser for Windows K-Meleon
- `xampp.zip` – portable environment for Windows supporting Apache Web Server and PHP, including ready-to-use **ELECTRONIC KNOWLEDGE SYSTEM ON TOXICOLOGY, ELECTRONIC KNOWLEDGE SYSTEM ON RENAISSANCE PAINTING, ELECTRONIC KNOWLEDGE SYSTEM ON LANGUAGE OF GESTURES, ELECTRONIC KNOWLEDGE SYSTEM ON AVITAMINOSIS**

2.2   IMK Interaction

The realization of **IMK** is based on idea of member of *USSR Academy of Science M. N. Livanov* [3] that the essence of memory associations is a spatial-temporal coherence of narrow-band periodical oscillations of central neurons sets activity.

Upon information input the list of propositions ranged by their value should be supplied.

Proposition Value Index PVI = $(E1/O1 + E2/O2)/2$

```
E1 = (referenced etalon elements/signs weights sum)
O1 = (object elements/signs number)
E2 = (referenced etalon elements/signs number)
O2 = (etalon elements/signs number)
 (Etalon description element/sign weight) = 1/ (number of etalons with
this element/sign).
```

The system assisting human expert's activity should comply with the following requirements described by *Arthur Conan Doyle* in *Sherlock Holmes* stories [10].

We would call it a knowledge machine.

Step 1 - Observation

1. A knowledge machine should have maximum possible information about a case before a judgment.

Step 2 - Producing propositions, based on knowledge

2. A knowledge machine should possess maximum possible knowledge in a sphere of implementation.
3. A knowledge machine should possess no excessive knowledge, should have nothing but the tools which may help in doing work.
4. Getting indication of the course of events, a knowledge machine should be able to guide itself by other similar cases which occur to its memory.
5. A knowledge machine should have an ability to take into account not only descriptions of situations in its memory but results as well, providing a possibility to reconstruct a description from a result, i.e. if you told it a result, it would be able to evolve what the steps were which led up to that result.
6. Possessing information about the great number of cases, a knowledge machine should have an ability to find a strong family resemblance about them, i.e. to find templates of typical cases.
7. A knowledge machine should have an ability to explain the grounds of its conclusion.
8. A knowledge machine should arrive at the conclusion for a few seconds after getting a description of case.
9. A knowledge machine should focus on the most unusual in descriptions of situations.

Step 3 - Elimination of impossible propositions

10. A knowledge machine should have an ability to point out all impossible propositions.

Step 4 - Selection and verification of the most appropriate propositions

11. A knowledge machine should estimate a level of a confidence of its propositions.

The technologies of **AI** as expert systems and neural networks don't comply with these requirements. And it is a reason why human-**AI** interaction is complicated at the time. People hardly can trust **AI** propositions.

Expert system [1] is based on the idea of decision tree, when, with every answer to a program's question, a direction of moving through a tree changes until a final leaf (decision) will be reached.

- So not all possible questions will be asked, and not maximum information will be received.
- The key elements are decision rules, but no knowledge itself. Not a word about the thousands of other similar cases, about typical cases.
- As we see, expert systems originally were designed to be deduction machines. But it is not very reliable to entrust to machine deciding what is absolutely impossible. We

think that more fruitful approach is to show what reasons to consider some hypotheses as impossible. And only man should make the final decision.

Neural network is based, as we know, on the idea of teaching of set of elements (neurons), controlling conductivity between them [2].

- A neural network cannot explain reasons of own conclusion in terms that people can understand. So it is very hard to verify its activity and, therefore, to believe.

An expert system is an example of a 'top-down' approach when particular instances of intelligent behavior selected and an attempt to design machines that can replicate that behavior was made. A neural network is an example of 'bottom-up' approach when there is an attempt to study the biological mechanisms that underlie human intelligence and to build machines, which work on similar principles.

IMK technology complies with all 11 requirements and unites 'top-down' and 'bottom-up' approaches. Any human knowledge written and spoken can be uploaded to **IMK** in a straight way by any expert not familiar with software coding. The **IMK** components are designed to create ready-to-use software application using simple text files edited by people. **IMK** assists intellectual activity, but does not replace people.

2.3 Building IMK Application

It is needed to prepare knowledge to be processed in a special human-like way.

Step I

You should name the project usually using up to 8 symbols suitable for file name (for example, **Renaissance Painting System** [9] may be named `renais`). Create a directory where system will reside, for example, `d:\renais`. Copy there the development software `soz2017b.exe`.

Preliminarily, it is needed to remove from initial text all excessive information, keeping titles, exact descriptions of situations and recommendations. Please try to concentrate on ideas rather than on words. We propose to define 'idea' as a standard text directly defining a specific side of a situation. You should control appearance of synonymous ideas, carefully removing duplications. Resulting text, which may be used as example, in a case of painting information, is the following.

```
1. Hieronimus Bosch (Van Aken), 1450-1516, Netherlands
----------------------------------------------------
Facial expressions are childlishly naive
...
```

Every idea in a description of situation we call a sign. In principle, any sign can have a grade, for example, if a sign is 'Weight' it may have grades '1-Very low, 2-Low, 3-Mean, 4-High, 5-Very high'. But in existing human texts all signs have as a rule only one grade. It is very rare need to use sign with several grades.

Step II

You should gather all signs from all descriptions of situations, eliminate duplicates, and number them pointing number of possible grades. You should make a file called, for example, renais.sgn of the following type.

```
1. Artist is pessimist (Sign's title up to 64 symbols)
1, (Number of sign's grades)
...
```

Step III

You should make a file called, for example, renais.stn, containing numbered titles of possible situations with numbers of corresponding signs and grades, where zero means end of list. If sign's grade is 1 than you may just place one more comma. It should look like the following.

```
1. Hieronimus Bosch (Van Aken), 1450-1516, Netherlands
1,,2,,3,,4,,5,,6,,7,,8,,9,,10,,11,,12,,13,,14,,15,,16,,17,,18,,
19,,115,,
0,,
2. Hieronimus Bosch, after 1500, Netherlands
20,,21,,22,,23,,24,,25,,26,,
0,,
3. Drawing by Hieronimus Bosch, 1450-1516, Netherlands
27,,28,,29,,30,,31,,
0,,
...
```

Step IV

You should make a file containing a questionnaire for a convenient description of a problem. In this questionnaire you should group questions regardless of its numbers. It is allowed to include additional explanations, if needed. Format of chapter's title is '== Title', format of sign's number is 'NNNN ~' (for example ' 11 ~ ') and format of sign's grade is 'NN ~ '. You should make a file called, for this example, renais.que of the following type.

```
== RENAISSANCE PAINTING
    General Knowledge Machine Research Group
(c) Copyright Konstantin M. Golubev 2017.
http://gkm-ekp.sf.net, gkm-ekp@users.sf.net
<em> Renaissance painting from Breughel to El Greco,
Text by Lionello Venturi, Translated by Stuart Gilbert,
(c) 1979 by Editions d'Art Albert Skira S.A., Geneva, ISBN 0 333 26644 7
</em>
<hr>
    DISCLAIMER WARNING!
This kind of system assists in paintings evaluation.
It shouldn't in no way replace qualified expert!
== PICTURE'S GENRE ===================================
    3 ~ Picture is in tradition of illuminators
    7 ~ Allegories with a moral purpose
...
```

Step V

You should make a file containing all propositions regarding identified situations. You should call it `renais.prp` and it should look like the following.

The first line of proposition is a title of situation from file `renais.stn` preceding by '~' sign. After this proposition text goes. Please note that for Internet version of e-knowledge system you may include any HTML tags into proposition text (references to pictures, multimedia, URL and so on).

```
~ 1. Hieronimus Bosch (Van Aken), 1450-1516
---------------------------------------------------------
  Artist is pessimist
  Artist saw not enough God presence in man
  Picture is in tradition of illuminators
  Painter is wholly medieval
  Fish, pigs, all kind of animals assume human-like forms
  Great number of small figures
  Allegories with a moral purpose
  Savage irony, which gives a piquancy
  Scene look like a puppet play
  Facial expressions are childlishly naive
  Artist was incapable of dramatic effects
  Stressing everywhere the conflict between good and evil
  A picture presents itself as a sequence in time
  Lightness of touch
  Airy freedom
  Exquisitely lovely figures dad in the most delicate of colors
  Color-light synthesis
  Tonal unity of the composition as a whole
  Deep religious sensibility
  Exceptionally fertile imagination
THE FOLLOWING IS DETAIL OF PICTURE "THE HAY WAGON", PRADO, MADRID
<IMG src="bosch.jpg">
...
```

Step VI

You should make a file called `soz2017b.ini` of the following format:

```
Title of e-knowledge system
Signs descriptions file name (.sgn)
Situations descriptions file name (.stn)
Propositions file name (.prp)
```

For example, in our system:

```
Electronic Knowledge System on Renaissance Painting
renais.sgn
renais.stn
renais.prp
```

Please run command interpreter. Change directory to that appointed for development. All previously created files must be placed in this directory. After that run the program soz2017b.exe. On completion view the file proto.soz. If it does not contain errors messages than initial e-knowledge base creation (files *.gkm) was successful. If there are errors please edit your files.

Initial sources have limitations: up to 2,000 possible signs, up to 8,000 possible situations (etalons), up to 100 signs in problem description, up to 100 signs in situation (etalon) description, up to 1,000 size of e-knowledge base element. It is sufficient to build very large e-knowledge system. But if it is necessary to build greater system, you should edit file all2017b.set and recompile sources.

Ready-to-use application development by component gkmforms.exe

Please run command interpreter. Change directory to that appointed for development. All previously created files must be placed in this directory. After that run the program gkmforms.exe.

Answer the name of project to question Title, for example, renais.

On completion view the file index.php that's a homepage for application like the following.

```
<!DOCTYPE HTML PUBLIC "-//IETF//DTD HTML 4//EN">
<html>
<head>
<META NAME = "description" CONTENT = "PAINTING">
<META NAME = "author" CONTENT = "GKM Research Group">
<META NAME = "keywords" CONTENT = "General Knowledge Machine, Online,
Electronic Knowledge Publishing, Intelligent Web Site, Intellect Modeling
Kit, GKM Research Group, Electronic Knowledge System">
<META HTTP-EQUIV="content-type" CONTENT="text/html; charset=windows-
1252">
<title>RENAISSANCE PAINTING</title>
</head>
<body bgcolor="#383853" link="#0000FF" VLINK="#0000ff" ALINK="#0000ff">
<a Name=YK><FORM ACTION="gkminter.php" METHOD=POST target='gkminterhtml'
NAME=gkmzf onSubmit='return ANSWER();'>
<table bgcolor="#FFFFFA" border=3 bordercolordark="#000001" cell-
padding=1 cellspacing=0>
<TR><TD align=left></a><STRONG>E-KNOWLEDGE SYSTEM</STRONG></TD><TD
align=right>Powered by General Knowledge Machine<A HREF=http://gkm-
ekp.sf.net><IMG SRC=gkmlogo.gif ALT='GKM Research Group Home' HSPACE=11
WIDTH=100 HEIGHT=53 ALIGN=TOP BORDER=0></A>IMG SRC=wgbhuser.gif ALT='Web
Access Symbol (for people with disabilities)' ALIGN=TOP BORDER=0></TD>
</TR><TR><TD><IMG SRC=Holmes.jpg alt='Mr Sherlock Holmes' align=left
border=1></TD><TD>
<EM><b>Disclaimer warning! This system is not a replacement of qualified
expert.<br>Authors should not be liable for any results of its implemen-
tation.<br>In every specific case only authorized person should make
decisions.</b></em><hr><br>
```

```
<B>RENAISSANCE PAINTING</B><br>
<br><INPUT NAME=Y1 TYPE=TEXT VALUE='Input here non-standard info like
name, title ...' SIZE=54><br><br>
<b>Please check all signs describing problem among listed below and press
(Advise).<br>Don't block pop-up window containing advice! Press
(Clear) to reset before next try. </b><br>
<br>Set higher Max. Prop. Num. if you need more results.  </b><br>
<BR><SELECT       NAME="SPISOK"       SIZE="1"       OnChange="SPISOKY()"
LANGUAGE="JAVASCRIPT">
<OPTION VALUE=1>INDEX OF CONTENTS
<OPTION VALUE=2>INDEPENDENT VERIFICATION PROJECT - CONSULTING POINT ON
PAINTING
<OPTION VALUE=3>PICTURE'S GENRE
<OPTION VALUE=4>PORTRAITS
<OPTION VALUE=5>HUMAN FIGURES
<OPTION VALUE=6>FIGURES
<OPTION VALUE=7>COLORS
<OPTION VALUE=8>LIGHT
...
```

On completion the files `renaisnnn.html` and `index.php` appear containing knowledge texts. For example:

`renais.html renais1.html ... renais31.html gkminter.php index.php`

You should create directory for application in `htdocs` directory of Apache Web server like `d:\xampp\htdocs\renais`. After that copy to it files `*.gkm`, `*.html`, `*.php`, `*.pdf`, `gkm2017b.exe`, `gkm2017b.ini`, and files from images directory. The address is `http://localhost:8000/renais`. The following is files list of **ELECTRONIC KNOWLEDGE SYSTEM ON RENAISSANCE PAINTING** (renais).

```
d:\xampp\htdocs\renais
boe.gkm db.gkm db2.gkm renais.html renais1.html... renais31.html gkm-n
gkm2017b.exe gkm2017b.ini gkmhelp.pdf gkminter.php gkmlogo.gif Holmes.
jpg i.e.gkm index.php ip.gkm oe.gkm seboe.gkm sip.gkm soe.gkm we.gkm
wgbhuser.gif
```

Ready-to-use applications provided

IMK includes the following application ready-to-use.

- **ELECTRONIC KNOWLEDGE SYSTEM ON TOXICOLOGY** (emergmed)
- **ELECTRONIC KNOWLEDGE SYSTEM ON RENAISSANCE PAINTING** (renais)
- **ELECTRONIC KNOWLEDGE SYSTEM ON LANGUAGE OF GESTURES** (gestures)
- **ELECTRONIC KNOWLEDGE SYSTEM ON AVITAMINOSIS** (avitamin)

They are located in the `htdocs` directory of `xampp` – portable environment for Windows supporting `Apache Web server` and `PHP`.

To install applications file xampp.zip should be unzipped into the root directory of partition, for example d:\xampp. The applications should be located in the following subdirectories of d:\xampp\htdocs - d:\xampp\htdocs\emergmed, d:\xampp\htdocs\renais, d:\xampp\htdocs\gestures and d:\xampp\htdocs\avitamin. Start Apache Web Server with command d:\xampp\apache_start.bat. A text window appears notifying about server start. Server shutdown is by closing a window.

The browser K-Meleon could be used for accessing applications. To install browser file kmeleon.zip should be unzipped into suitable directory, for example, d:\K-MeleonPortable. Start browser with command d:\K-MeleonPortable\K-MeleonPortable.exe. The initial page pointing to presented applications appears, for example, http://localhost:8000.

2.4 Natural Cluster Analysis

Have you ever tried to understand is there any sense in a significant amount of data? Did you use heavy mathematics to classify objects? Was it easy and convenient?

Have you been satisfied with results?

Amazingly, but human experts can do such a job without any mathematics. We call such persons experienced. They know not only facts but can explain relations between facts, set general cases and rules for their treatment.

Can we develop mathematics to simulate this?

Let us try to solve the following problem with theoretical mathematics. We have 1000 cases with every case described by subset of parameters from a whole set of parameters with total number 1000. We want to find typical cases dividing all number of cases into groups of similar ones.

How we can do this?

We can place all cases into the database and try to query database with all possible subsets of parameters. This way we hope to find typical combinations of parameters and corresponding groups of cases.

What computing power we will need?

The most powerful supercomputer in the world of 2016 Tianhe-2 (54 PFLOPS) has the power of $6*10^{16}$ FLOPS (Floating point operations per second). It is equal approximately to 2^{50} FLOPS. Assume that we can do one query per one FLOP. In reality it takes much more. Total number of queries should be 2^{1000}. The time needed is $(2^{1000})/(2^{50}) = 2^{950}$, i.e. 10^{300} s. This number is really greater than number of seconds in universe existence, i.e. $4.32*10^{17}$.

But could we simulate human tactics?

The brain contains near 100 billion neurons, every one of them is a computer. They are working together in an organized way and it is impossible at the moment to build such a complex structure.

Is situation hopeless?

The brain is multi-floor building and what we know about intellect is higher floor expressed by words. Fortunately, number of verbal concepts and ideas used by people are limited and can be replicated by our computers.

How?

If we could model intellectual activity based on verbal ideas, then we would have a chance to simulate human experience.

The central point of this is ability of human brain to find similar objects descriptions inside memory. The brain can do it almost instantly.

The IMK technology may be used to simulate this activity. With this technology it is possible to model expert evaluation of situation based on human knowledge doing grouping/categorization. Every object from set should belong to at least one group. And all objects in group should be similar.

We can start the following procedure. With General Knowledge Machine we try to find for every object sets of similar objects in a chosen range of similarity limits and compute signs typical for thus found groups with a given frequency of occurrence. After that we build groups of objects containing all or almost all found signs. This way we have number of compound iterations equal to a number of initial objects. And the time needed is moderate, usually hours.

It is possible that not all groups can be found this way but many of them could. And we have a possibility to set some signs as obligatory that provides very convenient thing. For example, we can set as obligatory signs treatment and result for a number of patients. And then we could see groups of typical patients having predefined treatment and result.

You should make a file called abs2017b.ini of the following format:

```
Title of e-knowledge system
Grades Dispersion Limit (%) [Start, Finish, Step]
(PVI) Similarity Limit [Start, Finish, Step]
(% Of Etalons) Regularity Signs Selection Limit (%) [Start, Finish, Step]
(Att. Ind. % of Signs) Group Selection Limit [Number]
(% of Objects in Group) Typical Signs Limit [Number]
Group Objects Number Lower Limit (%) [Number]
Obligatory Signs. Up to 10 [Number]
```

For example, in our system:

```
Renais
0,0,0,
1,98,1,
1,98,1,
80,
85,
5,
0
```

Please run command interpreter. Change directory to that appointed for development. All previously created files must be placed in this directory. After that run the program abs2017b.exe.

Answer the name of project to question Title, for example, renais. Input values into appropriate fields.

On completion view the file proto.abs.

You can look at variant of proto.abs in sources for **Renaissance Painting**.

Intellect Modeling Kit v.2017beta regularities finding
Copyright (C) 1987-2017 Konstantin M. Golubev
http://gkm-ekp.sf.net, gkm-ekp@users.sf.net
Distributed under Lesser GNU General Public License
Snum: 2000 Enum: 8000 Emax:100 Imax:100 Base: 1000 Sn: 80 En: 80
Renaissance Painting
Regularities Finding

***** Signs Probabilities *****
  Total Number of Etalons 31
    3. % 1)1. Artist is pessimist
    3. % 2)2. Artist saw not enough God presence in man
    3. % 3)3. Picture is in tradition of illuminators
...
**** Regularity derived from the object:
    18.18. Jacomo Pontormo (Carrucci), 1494-1556/57, Tuscany, Italy
    204 - 1)204. Mannerist
    226 - 1)226. Elongation of proportions
    231 - 1)231. Anti-classical composition
  Group members
      23.23. Niccolo dell'Abbate, 1509-1571, Modena, Italy
      30.30. El Greco (Domenikos Theotokopulos), 1541-1614, Italy, Spain
  Total 2 of 31 (6.45 +- 8.65%)
**** Regularity derived from the object:
    18.18. Jacomo Pontormo (Carrucci), 1494-1556/57, Tuscany, Italy
    204 - 1)204. Mannerist
    226 - 1)226. Elongation of proportions
  Group members
      22.22. Francesco Parmigianino (Mazzda), 1503-1540, Parma, Italy
      23.23. Niccolo dell'Abbate, 1509-1571, Modena, Italy
      30.30. El Greco (Domenikos Theotokopulos), 1541-1614, Italy, Spain
  Total 3 of 31 (9.68 +- 10.41%)
**** Regularity derived from the object:
    19.19. Rosso Fiorentino (Giovanni Battista), 1495-1540, Florence
    204 - 1)204. Mannerist
  Group members
      18.18. Jacomo Pontormo (Carrucci), 1494-1556/57, Tuscany, Italy
      19.19. Rosso Fiorentino (Giovanni Battista), 1495-1540, Florence
      20.20. Domenico Beccafumi, 1486-1551, Montaperti, Italy
      21.21. Agnolo Bronzino (di Cosimo), 1503-1572, Florence, Italy
      22.22. Francesco Parmigianino (Mazzda), 1503-1540, Parma, Italy
      23.23. Niccolo dell'Abbate, 1509-1571, Modena, Italy
      28.28. Bartholomeus Spranger, 1546-1611, Netherlands
      29.29. Pieter Aertsen, 1508-1575, Netherlands
      30.30. El Greco (Domenikos Theotokopulos), 1541-1614, Italy, Spain

Total 9 of 31 (29.03 +- 15.98%)
**** Regularity derived from the object:
   15.15. Tintoretto (Jacopo Robusti), 1518-1594, Venetia
   115 - 1)115. Exceptionally fertile imagination
   Group members
      1. 1. Hieronimus Bosch (Van Aken), 1450-1516, Netherlands
      15.15. Tintoretto (Jacopo Robusti), 1518-1594, Venetia
      19.19. Rosso Fiorentino (Giovanni Battista), 1495-1540, Florence
   Total 3 of 31 (9.68 +- 10.41%)
**** Regularity derived from the object:
   4. 4. Quentin Massys, 1466-1530, Netherlands
   39 - 1)39. Total serenity
   40 - 1)40. Depicting man and nature with loving care in details
   41 - 1)41. Color are conditioned by the images, not autonomous
   Group members
      4. 4. Quentin Massys, 1466-1530, Netherlands
      5. 5. Eyckian tradition, Netherlands
   Total 2 of 31 (6.45 +- 8.65%)
**** Regularity derived from the object:
   7. 7. Pieter Brueghel, 1525/30-1569, Netherlands
   13 - 1)13. A picture presents itself as a sequence in time
   Group members
      1. 1. Hieronimus Bosch (Van Aken), 1450-1516, Netherlands
      7. 7. Pieter Brueghel, 1525/30-1569, Netherlands
   Total 2 of 31 (6.45 +- 8.65%)
**** Regularity derived from the object:
   24.24. Francois Clouet, before 1522-1572, France
   233 - 1)233. Attention to details
   Group members
      24.24. Francois Clouet, before 1522-1572, France
      27.27. Antonio Moro, 1519-1576, Netherlands
   Total 2 of 31 (6.45 +- 8.65%)
******* GROUPS FOUND ***********

2.5   Software Compilation

IMK supplied with sources and binaries for Windows and Linux. Portable Windows GNU Fortran gfortran4.zip and Free Basic compilers freebas.zip are included. Universal Windows IDE GEANY is included in geany.zip.

In order to compile for your system e-knowledge base engine provide that GNU compiler is on your system (visit http://www.gnu.org). Unzip, for example, GNU Fortran compiler to directory d:\gfortran4, Free Basic compiler to directory d:\FreeBASIC-1.04.0-win32 (Figs. 1, 2 and 3).

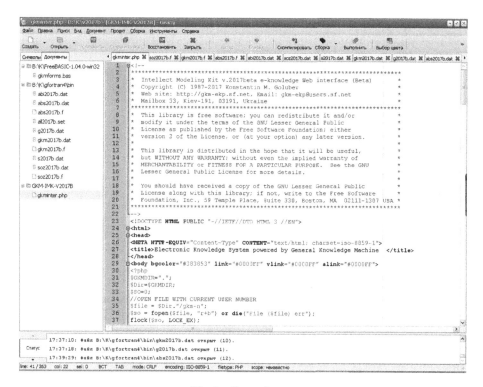

Fig. 1. Geany layout

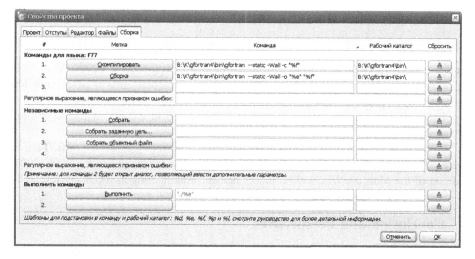

Fig. 2. Geany Fortran settings

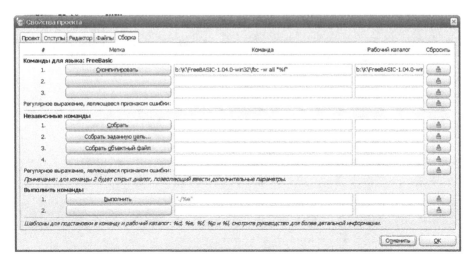

Fig. 3. Geany FreeBasic settings

Unzip Fortran sources `*.f`, `*.dat`, `*.set` to selected directory with compiler binary like `d:\gfortran4\bin`. Change directory to chosen one. Issue commands:

```
gfortran soz2017b.f -o soz2017b.exe
gfortran gkm2017b.f -o gkm2017b.exe
gfortran abs2017b.f -o abs2017b.exe
```

Unzip Free Basic sources *.bas to selected directory with compiler binary like `d:\FreeBASIC-1.04.0-win32`. Change directory to chosen one. Issue command:

```
fbc -w all gkmforms.bas
```

2.6   Results

Early versions of General Knowledge Machine were developed for UNIX, MS-DOS, Windows operating systems. The latest version supports all platforms of GNU compiler options (any Windows, Linux, UNIX…).

There are working products which can be presented to experts in corresponding areas.

Products were tested in various environments – business, medicine, arts. Papers were published in Russia, Italy and UK [4]. The work was featured in the 2006–2007 Edition of the Marquis Who's Who in Science and Engineering as a pioneer research.

3   Conclusion and Perspectives

Some people say about a crisis of human intellect. Of course, it is not so. May be it's a crisis of human self-confidence. In the beginning there were many promises to built machines more intelligent than people. And those machines should use advanced principles of work, much better than obsolete human intellect [5]. Instead of help to human intellect there were attempts to replace it. But those, who read works of academician V. Vernadsky from Ukraine [6], E. Le Roy [7] and P. Teilhard de Chardin from France [8], know that the main result of evolution on Earth is creation of Noosphere - a sphere of intellect. And, in this case, it is very interesting what can be called an intellect, but is based on other principles than developed by evolution?

Acknowledgements. The author is deeply grateful to Head of IFIP TC12 Artificial Intelligence Technical Committee Professor Eunika Mercier-Laurent for extremely valuable support and very encouraging attitude.

References

1. Alty, J.L., Coombs, M.J.: Expert systems. Concepts and examples. The National Computing Centre Limited, Manchester (1984)
2. Hinton, G.E.: Learning in Parallel Networks. Byte. McGraw-Hill, Inc., New York (1985)
3. Livanov, M.N.: Spatial Organization of Cerebral Processes. Wiley, Chichester (1977)
4. Golubev, K.M.: Adaptive learning with e-knowledge systems. IJTM **25**(6/7), 553–559 (2003)
5. Schank, R., Hunter, L.: The quest to understand thinking. Byte. McGraw-Hill, Inc., New York (1985)
6. Vernadsky, V.I.: The Biosphere. Translated by Langmuir, D.B., McMenamin, M.A.S. (ed.). Copernicus, New York (1998)
7. Le Roy, E.: Les origines humaines et l'evolution de l'intelligence. Paris (1928)
8. Teilhard de Chardin, P.: La place de l'homme dans la nature. Éditions du Seuil, Paris (1956)
9. Venturi, L.: Renaissance painting from Breughel to El Greco. Translated by Gilbert, S. Editions d'Art Albert Skira S.A., Geneva (1979)
10. Doyle, S.A.C.: The Penguin Complete Sherlock Holmes. With a preface of Christopher Morley. Penguin Books, London (1981)

Author Index

Printed in the United States
by Baker & Taylor Publisher Services